RADICAL CHIC & MAU-MAUING THE FLAK CATCHERS
&
THE PAINTED WORD

Tom Wolfe is the author of more than a dozen books, among them such contemporary classics as *The Electric Kool-Acid Test*, *The Right Stuff*, *The Bonfire of the Vanities* and *A Man in Full*. A native of Richmond, Virginia, he earned his B.A. at Washington and Lee University and a Ph.D. in American studies at Yale. He lives in New York City.

Also by Tom Wolfe

Tom Wolfe

Radical Chic & Mau-Mauing the Flak Catchers

&

The Painted Word

PICADOR

Radical Chic & Mau-Mauing the Flak Catchers first published 1970
by Farrar, Straus & Giroux

The Painted Word first published 1975 by Harper's Magazine
First published in book form 1975 by Farrar, Straus & Giroux

This combined edition published 2002 by Picador
an imprint of Pan Macmillan Ltd
Pan Macmillan, 20 New Wharf Road, London N1 9RR
Basingstoke and Oxford
Associated companies throughout the world
www.panmacmillan.com

ISBN 0 330 49372 8

1 3 5 7 9 8 6 4 2

A CIP catalogue record for this book is available from
the British Library.

Printed and bound in Great Britain by
Mackays of Chatham plc, Chatham, Kent

Radical Chic & Mau-Mauing the Flak Catchers

Radical Chic

AT 2 OR 3 OR 4 A.M., SOMEWHERE ALONG IN THERE, ON August 25, 1966, his forty-eighth birthday, in fact, Leonard Bernstein woke up in the dark in a state of wild alarm. That had happened before. It was one of the forms his insomnia took. So he did the usual. He got up and walked around a bit. He felt groggy. Suddenly he had a vision, an inspiration. He could see himself, Leonard Bernstein, the *egregio maestro,* walking out on stage in white tie and tails in front of a full orchestra. On one side of the conductor's podium is a piano. On the other is a chair with a guitar leaning against it. He sits in the chair and picks up the guitar. A guitar! One of those half-witted instruments, like the accordion, that are made for the Learn-to-Play-in-Eight-Days E-Z-Diagram 110-IQ fourteen-year-olds of Levittown! But there's a reason. He has an anti-war message to deliver to this great starched white-throated audience in the symphony hall. He announces to them: "I love." Just that. The effect is mortifying. All at once a Negro rises up from out of the curve of the grand piano and starts saying things like, "The audience is curiously embarrassed." Lenny tries to start again, plays some quick numbers on the piano, says, "I love. *Amo ergo sum.*" The Negro rises again and says, "The audience thinks he ought to get up and walk out. The audience thinks, 'I am ashamed even to nudge my neighbor.' " Finally, Lenny gets off a heartfelt anti-war speech and exits.

For a moment, sitting there alone in his home in the small hours of the morning, Lenny thought it might just work and he jotted the idea down. Think of the headlines: BERNSTEIN ELECTRIFIES CONCERT AUDIENCE WITH ANTI-WAR APPEAL. But then his enthusiasm collapsed. He lost heart. Who the hell was this Negro rising up from the piano and informing the world what an ass Leonard Bernstein was making of himself? It didn't make sense, this superego Negro by the concert grand.

MMMMMMMMMMMMMMMM. THESE ARE NICE. LITTLE ROQUE-fort cheese morsels rolled in crushed nuts. Very tasty. Very subtle. It's the way the dry sackiness of the nuts tiptoes up against the dour savor of the cheese that is so nice, so subtle. Wonder what the Black Panthers eat here on the hors d'oeuvre trail? Do the Panthers like little Roquefort cheese morsels rolled in crushed nuts this way, and asparagus tips in mayonnaise dabs, and *meatballs petites au Coq Hardi,* all of which are at this very moment being offered to them on gadrooned silver platters by maids in black uniforms with hand-ironed white aprons . . . The butler will bring them their drinks . . . Deny it if you wish to, but such are the *pensées méta-physiques* that rush through one's head on these Radical Chic evenings just now in New York. For example, does that huge Black Panther there in the hallway, the one shaking hands with Felicia Bernstein herself, the one with the black leather coat and the dark glasses and the absolutely unbelievable Afro, Fuzzy-Wuzzy-scale, in fact—is he, a Black Panther, going on to pick up a Roquefort cheese morsel rolled in crushed nuts from off the tray, from a maid in uniform, and just pop it down the gullet without so much as missing a beat of Felicia's perfect Mary Astor voice . . .

Felicia is remarkable. She is beautiful, with that rare bur-nished beauty that lasts through the years. Her hair is pale blond and set just so. She has a voice that is "theatrical," to use a term from her youth. She greets the Black Panthers with the same bend of the wrist, the same tilt of the head, the same per-fect Mary Astor voice with which she greets people like Jason, John and D.D., Adolph, Betty, Gian-Carlo, Schuyler, and Goddard, during those *après*-concert suppers she and Lenny are so famous for. What evenings! She lights the candles over the dining-room table, and in the Gotham gloaming the little tremulous tips of flame are reflected in the mirrored surface of the table, a bottomless blackness with a thousand stars, and it is that moment that Lenny loves. There seem to be a thousand stars above and a thousand stars below, a room full of stars, a penthouse duplex full of stars, a Manhattan tower full of stars, with marvelous people drifting through the heavens, Jason Robards, John and D. D. Ryan, Gian-Carlo Menotti, Schuyler Chapin, Goddard Lieberson, Mike Nichols, Lillian Hellman, Larry Rivers, Aaron Copland, Richard Avedon, Milton and Amy Greene, Lukas Foss, Jennie Tourel, Samuel Barber,

Jerome Robbins, Steve Sondheim, Adolph and Phyllis Green, Betty Comden, and the Patrick O'Neals ...

... and now, in the season of Radical Chic, the Black Panthers. That huge Panther there, the one Felicia is smiling her tango smile at, is Robert Bay, who just forty-one hours ago was arrested in an altercation with the police, supposedly over a .38-caliber revolver that someone had, in a parked car in Queens at Northern Boulevard and 104th Street or some such unbelievable place, and taken to jail on a most unusual charge called "criminal facilitation." And now he is out on bail and walking into Leonard and Felicia Bernstein's thirteen-room penthouse duplex on Park Avenue. Harassment & Hassles, Guns & Pigs, Jail & Bail—they're *real,* these Black Panthers. The very idea of them, these real revolutionaries, who actually put their lives on the line, runs through Lenny's duplex like a rogue hormone. Everyone casts a glance, or stares, or tries a smile, and then sizes up the house for the somehow delicious counterpoint ... Deny it if you want to! but one *does* end up making such sweet furtive comparisons in this season of Radical Chic ... There's Otto Preminger in the library and Jean vanden Heuvel in the hall, and Peter and Cheray Duchin in the living room, and Frank and Domna Stanton, Gail Lumet, Sheldon Harnick, Cynthia Phipps, Burton Lane, Mrs. August Heckscher, Roger Wilkins, Barbara Walters, Bob Silvers, Mrs. Richard Avedon, Mrs. Arthur Penn, Julie Belafonte, Harold Taylor, and scores more, including Charlotte Curtis, women's news editor of *The New York Times,* America's foremost chronicler of Society, a lean woman in black, with her notebook out, standing near Felicia and big Robert Bay, and talking to Cheray Duchin.

Cheray tells her: "I've never met a Panther—this is a first

for me!" . . . never dreaming that within forty-eight hours her words will be on the desk of the President of the United States . . .

This is a first for me. But she is not alone in her thrill as the Black Panthers come trucking on in, into Lenny's house, Robert Bay, Don Cox the Panthers' Field Marshal from Oakland, Henry Miller the Harlem Panther defense captain, the Panther women—Christ, if the Panthers don't know how to get it all together, as they say, the tight pants, the tight black turtlenecks, the leather coats, Cuban shades, Afros. But real Afros, not the ones that have been shaped and trimmed like a topiary hedge and sprayed until they have a sheen like acrylic wall-to-wall—but like funky, natural, scraggly . . . wild . . .

These are no civil-rights Negroes *wearing gray suits three sizes too big—*

—no more interminable Urban League banquets in hotel ballrooms where they try to alternate the blacks and whites around the tables as if they were stringing Arapaho beads—

—*these are* real men!

Shoot-outs, revolutions, pictures in *Life* magazine of policemen grabbing Black Panthers like they were Vietcong—somehow it all runs together in the head with the whole thing of how *beautiful* they are. *Sharp as a blade.* The Panther women—there are three or four of them on hand, wives of the Panther 21 defendants, and they are so lean, so *lithe,* as they say, with tight pants and Yoruba-style headdresses, almost like turbans, as if they'd stepped out of the pages of *Vogue,* although no doubt *Vogue* got it from them. All at once every woman in the room knows exactly what Amanda Burden meant when she said she was now anti-fashion because "the sophistication of the baby blacks made me rethink my attitudes." God knows the Panther women don't spend thirty minutes in front of the mirror in the morning shoring up their eye holes with contact lenses, eyeliner, eye shadow, eyebrow pencil, occipital rim brush, false eyelashes, mascara, Shadow-Ban for undereye and Eterna Creme for the corners . . . And here they are, right in front of you, trucking on into the Bernsteins' Chinese yellow duplex, amid the sconces, silver bowls full of white and lavender anemones, and uniformed servants serving drinks and Roquefort cheese morsels rolled in crushed nuts—

But it's all right. They're *white* servants, not Claude and Maude, but white South Americans. Lenny and Felicia are geniuses. After a while, it all comes down to servants. They are the cutting edge in Radical Chic. Obviously, if you are giving a party for the Black Panthers, as Lenny and Felicia are this evening, or as Sidney and Gail Lumet did last week, or as John Simon of Random House and Richard Baron, the publisher, did before that; or for the Chicago Eight, such as the party Jean vanden Heuvel gave; or for the grape workers or Bernadette Devlin, such as the parties Andrew Stein gave; or for the Young Lords, such as the party Ellie Guggenheimer is giving next week in *her* Park Avenue duplex; or for the Indians or the SDS or the G.I. coffee shops or even for the Friends of the Earth—well, then, obviously you can't have a Negro butler and maid, Claude and Maude, in uniform, circulating through the living room, the library, and the main hall serving drinks and canapés. Plenty of people have tried to think it out. They try to picture the Panthers or whoever walking in bristling with electric hair and Cuban shades and leather pieces and the rest of it, and they try to picture Claude and Maude with the black uniforms coming up and saying,

"Would you care for a drink, sir?" They close their eyes and try to picture it *some way,* but there *is* no way. One simply cannot see that moment. So the current wave of Radical Chic has touched off the most desperate search for white servants. Carter and Amanda Burden have white servants. Sidney Lumet and his wife Gail, who is Lena Horne's daughter, have three white servants, including a Scottish nurse. Everybody has white servants. And Lenny and Felicia—they had it worked out before Radical Chic even started. Felicia grew up in Chile. Her father, Roy Elwood Cohn, an engineer from San Francisco, worked for the American Smelting and Refining Co. in Santiago. As Felicia Montealegre (her mother's maiden name), she became an actress in New York and won the *Motion Picture Daily* critics' award as the best new television actress of 1949. Anyway, they have a house staff of three white South American servants, including a Chilean cook, plus Lenny's English chauffeur and dresser, who is also white, of course. Can one comprehend how perfect that is, given . . . the times? Well, many of their friends can, and they ring up the Bernsteins and ask them to get South American servants for them, and the Bernsteins are so generous about it, so obliging, that people refer to them, good-naturedly and gratefully, as "the Spic and Span Employment Agency," with an easygoing ethnic humor, of course.

The only other thing to do is what Ellie Guggenheimer is doing next week with her party for the Young Lords in her duplex on Park Avenue at 89th Street, just ten blocks up from Lenny and Felicia. She is giving her party on a Sunday, which is the day off for the maid and the cleaning woman. "Two friends of mine"—she confides on the telephone—"two friends of mine who happen to be . . . not white—that's what I hate about the times we live in, the *terms*—well, they've agreed to be butler and maid . . . and I'm going to be a maid myself!"

Just at this point some well-meaning soul is going to say, Why not do without servants altogether if the matter creates such unbearable tension and one truly believes in equality? Well, even to raise the question is to reveal the most fundamental ignorance of life in the great co-ops and townhouses of the East Side in the age of Radical Chic. Why, my God! servants are not a mere convenience, they're an absolute psychological necessity. Once one is into that life, truly into it, with the morning workout on the velvet swings at Kounovsky's and the late mornings on the telephone, and lunch at the Running Footman, which is now regarded as really better than La Grenouille, Lutèce, Lafayette, La Caravelle, and the rest of the general Frog Pond, less ostentatious, more of the David Hicks feeling, less of the Parish-Hadley look, and then—well, then, the idea of not having servants is unthinkable. But even that does not say it all. It makes it sound like a matter of convenience, when actually it is a sheer and fundamental matter of—*having servants*. Does one comprehend?

God, what a flood of taboo thoughts runs through one's head at these Radical Chic events . . . But it's delicious. It is as if one's nerve endings were on red alert to the most intimate nuances of status. Deny it if you want to! Nevertheless, it runs through every soul here. It is the matter of the marvelous contradictions on all sides. It is like the delicious shudder you get when you try to force the prongs of two horseshoe magnets together . . . *them* and *us* . . .

For example, one's own servants, although white, are generally no problem. A discreet, euphemistic word about what sort of party it is going to be, and they will generally be models of correctness. The euphemisms are not always an easy matter, however. When talking to one's white servants, one doesn't really know whether to refer to blacks as *blacks, Negroes,* or *colored people.* When talking to other . . . well, *cultivated* persons, one says *blacks,* of course. It is the only word, currently, that implicitly shows one's awareness of the dignity of the black race. But somehow when you start to say the word to your own white servants, you hesitate. You can't get it out of your throat. Why? *Counter-guilt!* You realize that you are about to utter one of those touchstone words that divide the cultivated from the uncultivated, the attuned from the unattuned, the *hip* from the dreary. As soon as the word comes out of your mouth—you know it before the first vocable pops on your lips—your own servant is going to size you up as one of those *limousine liberals,* or whatever epithet they use, who are busy pouring white soul all over the black movement, and would you do as much for the white lower class, for the domestics of the East Side, for example, fat chance, sahib. Deny it if you want to! but such are the delicious little agonies of Radical Chic. So one settles for *Negro,* with the hope that the great god Culturatus has laid the ledger aside for the moment. . . . In any case, if one is able to make that small compromise, one's own servants are no real problem. But the elevator man and the doorman—the death rays they begin projecting, the curt responses, as soon as they see it is going to be one of *those* parties! Of course, they're all from Queens, and so forth, and one has to allow for that. For some reason the elevator men tend to be worse about it than the doormen, even; less sense of *politesse,* perhaps.

Or—what does one wear to these parties for the Panthers or the Young Lords or the grape workers? What does a woman wear? Obviously one does not want to wear something frivolously and pompously expensive, such as a Gerard Pipart party dress. On the other hand one does not want to arrive "poormouthing it" in some outrageous turtleneck and West Eighth Street bell-jean combination, as if one is "funky" and of "the people." Frankly, Jean vanden Heuvel—that's Jean there in the hallway giving everyone her famous smile, in which her eyes narrow down to f/16—frankly, Jean tends too much toward the funky fallacy. Jean, who is the daughter of Jules Stein, one of the wealthiest men in the country, is wearing some sort of rust-red snap-around suede skirt, the sort that English working girls pick up on Saturday afternoons in those absolutely *berserk* London boutiques like Bus Stop or Biba, where everything looks chic and yet skimpy and raw and vital. Felicia Bernstein seems to understand the whole thing better. Look at Felicia. She is wearing the simplest little black frock imaginable, with absolutely no ornamentation save for a plain gold necklace. It is perfect. It has dignity without any overt class symbolism.

Lenny? Lenny himself has been in the living room all this time, talking to old friends like the Duchins and the Stantons and the Lanes. Lenny is wearing a black turtleneck, navy blazer, Black Watch plaid trousers, and a necklace with a pendant hanging down to his sternum. His tailor comes here to the apartment to take the measurements and do the fittings. Lenny is a short, trim man, and yet he always seems tall. It is his head. He has a noble head, with a face that is at once sensitive and rugged, and a full stand of iron-gray hair, with sideburns, all set off nicely by the Chinese yellow of the room. His success radiates from his eyes and his smile with a charm that illustrates Lord Jersey's adage that "contrary to what the

Methodists tell us, money and success are good for the soul."
Lenny may be fifty-one, but he is still the *Wunderkind* of
American music. Everyone says so. He is not only one of the
world's outstanding conductors, but a more than competent
composer and pianist as well. He is the man who more than
any other has broken down the wall between elite music and
popular tastes, with *West Side Story* and his children's concerts
on television. How natural that he should stand here in his
own home radiating the charm and grace that make him an
easy host for leaders of the oppressed. How ironic that the next
hour should prove so shattering for this *egregio maestro*! How
curious that the Negro by the piano should emerge tonight!

A BELL RANG, A DINNER-TABLE BELL, BY THE SOUND OF IT,
the sort one summons the maid out of the kitchen with, and
the party shifted from out of the hall and into the living room.
Felicia led the way, Felicia and a small gray man, with gray
hair, a gray face, a gray suit, and a pair of Groovy but gray
sideburns. A little gray man, in short, who would be popping
up at key moments . . . to keep the freight train of history on
the track, as it were . . .

Felicia was down at the far end of the living room trying to
coax everybody in.

"Lenny!" she said. "Tell the fringes to come on in!" Lenny
was still in the back of the living room, near the hall.
"Fringes!" said Lenny. "Come on in!"

In the living room most of the furniture, the couches, easy
chairs, side tables, side chairs, and so on, had been pushed toward the walls, and thirty or forty folding chairs were set up in
the middle of the floor. It was a big, wide room with Chinese
yellow walls and white moldings, sconces, pier-glass mirrors, a

portrait of Felicia reclining on a summer chaise, and at the far end, where Felicia was standing, a pair of grand pianos. A pair of them; the two pianos were standing back to back, with the tops down and their bellies swooping out. On top of both pianos was a regular flotilla of family photographs in silver frames, the kind of pictures that stand straight up thanks to little velvet- or moiré-covered buttresses in the back, the kind that decorators in New York recommend to give a living room a homelike lived-in touch. "The million-dollar *chatchka* look," they call it. In a way it was perfect for Radical Chic. The nice part was that with Lenny it was instinctive; with Felicia, too. The whole place looked as if the inspiration had been to spend a couple of hundred thousand on the interior without looking pretentious, although that is no great sum for a thirteen-room co-op, of course . . . Imagine explaining all that to the Black Panthers. It was another delicious thought . . . The sofas, for example, were covered in the fashionable splashy prints on a white background covering deep downy cushions, in the Billy Baldwin or Margaret Owen tradition—without it looking like Billy or Margaret had been in there fussing about with teapoys and japanned chairs. *Gemütlich* . . . Old Vienna when Grandpa was alive . . . That was the ticket . . .

Once Lenny got "the fringes" moving in, the room filled up rapidly. It was jammed, in fact. People were sitting on sofas and easy chairs along the sides, as well as on the folding chairs, and were standing in the back, where Lenny was. Otto Preminger was sitting on a sofa down by the pianos, where the speakers were going to stand. The Panther wives were sitting in the first two rows with their Yoruba headdresses on, along with Henry Mitchell and Julie Belafonte, Harry Belafonte's wife. Julie is white, but they all greeted her warmly as "Sister."

Behind her was sitting Barbara Walters, hostess of the *Today Show* on television, wearing a checked pants suit with a great fluffy fur collar on the coat. Harold Taylor, the former "Boy President" of Sarah Lawrence, now fifty-five and silver-haired, but still youthful-looking, came walking down toward the front and gave a hug and a big social kiss to Gail Lumet. Robert Bay settled down in the middle of the folding chairs. Jean vanden Heuvel stood in the back and sought to focus . . . f/16 . . . on the pianos . . . Charlotte Curtis stood beside the door, taking notes.

And then Felicia stood up beside the pianos and said: "I want to thank you all very, very much for coming. I'm very, very glad to see so many of you here." Everything was fine. Her voice was rich as a woodwind. She introduced a man named Leon Quat, a lawyer involved in raising funds for the Panther 21, twenty-one Black Panthers who had been arrested on a charge of conspiring to blow up five New York department stores, New Haven Railroad facilities, a police station, and the Bronx Botanical Gardens.

Leon Quat, oddly enough, had the general look of those fifty-two-year-old men who run a combination law office, real estate, and insurance operation on the second floor of a two-story taxpayer out on Queens Boulevard. And yet that wasn't the kind of man Leon Quat really was. He had the sideburns. Quite a pair. They didn't come down just to the intertragic notch, which is that little notch in the lower rim of the ear, and which so many tentative Swingers aim their sideburns toward. No, on top of this complete Queens Boulevard insurance-agent look, he had real sideburns, to the bottom of the lobe, virtual muttonchops, which somehow have become the mark of the Movement.

Leon Quat rose up smiling: "We are very grateful to Mrs. Bernstein"—only he pronounced it "steen."

"STEIN!"—a great smoke-cured voice booming out from the rear of the room! It's Lenny! Leon Quat and the Black Panthers will have a chance to hear from Lenny. That much is sure. He is on the case. Leon Quat must be the only man in the room who does not know about Lenny and the Mental Jotto at 3 a.m. . . . For years, twenty at the least, Lenny has insisted on *-stein* not *-steen,* as if to say, I am not one of those 1921 Jews who try to tone down their Jewishness by watering their names down with a bad soft English pronunciation. Lenny has made such a point of *-stein* not *-steen,* in fact, that some people in this room think at once of the story of how someone approached Larry Rivers, the artist, and said, "What's this I hear about you and Leonard Bernstein"—*steen,* he pronounced it—"not speaking to each other any more?"—to which Rivers said, *"STEIN!"*

"We are very grateful . . . for her marvelous hospitality," says Quat, apparently not wanting to try the name again right away.

Then he beams toward the crowd: "I assume we are all just an effete clique of snobs and intellectuals in this room . . . I am referring to the words of Vice-President Agnew, of course, who can't be with us today because he is in the South Pacific explaining the Nixon doctrine to the Australians. All vice-presidents suffer from the Avis complex—they're second best, so they try harder, like General Ky or Hubert Humphrey . . ." He keeps waiting for the grins and chuckles after each of these mots, but all the celebrities and culturati are nonplussed. They give him a kind of dumb attention. They came here for the Panthers and Radical Chic, and here is Old Queens Boulevard

Real Estate Man with sideburns on telling them Agnew jokes. But Quat is too deep into his weird hole to get out. "Whatever respect I have had for Lester Maddox, I lost it when I saw Humphrey put his arm around his shoulder..." and somehow Quat begins disappearing down a hole bunging Hubert Humphrey with lumps of old Shelley Berman material. Slowly he climbs back out. He starts telling about the oppression of the Panther 21. They have been in jail since April 2, 1969, awaiting trial on ludicrous charges such as conspiring to blow up the Bronx Botanical Gardens. Their bail has been a preposterous $100,000 per person, which has in effect denied them the right to bail. They have been kept split up and moved from jail to jail. For all intents and purposes they have been denied the right to confer with their lawyers to prepare a defense. They have been subjected to inhuman treatment in jail—such as the case of Lee Berry, an epileptic, who was snatched out of a hospital bed and thrown in jail and kept in solitary confinement with a light bulb burning over his head night and day. The Panthers who have not been thrown in jail or killed, like Fred Hampton, are being stalked and harassed everywhere they go. "One of the few higher officials who is still . . . in the clear"—Quat smiles—"is here today. Don Cox, Field Marshal of the Black Panther Party."

"Right on," a voice says to Leon Quat, rather softly. And a tall black man rises from behind one of Lenny's grand pianos... *The Negro by the piano* ...

THE FIELD MARSHAL OF THE BLACK PANTHER PARTY HAS been sitting in a chair between the piano and the wall. He rises up; he has the hard-rock look, all right; he is a big tall man with brown skin and an Afro and a goatee and a black turtleneck much like Lenny's, and he stands up beside the piano, next to Lenny's million-dollar *chatchka* flotilla of family photographs. In fact, there is a certain perfection as the first Black Panther rises within a Park Avenue living room to lay the Panthers' ten-point program on New York Society in the age of Radical Chic. Cox is silhouetted—well, about nineteen feet behind him is a white silk shade with an Empire scallop over one of the windows overlooking Park Avenue. Or maybe it isn't silk, but a Jack Lenor Larsen mercerized cotton, something like that, lustrous but more subtle than silk. The whole image, the white shade and the Negro by the piano silhouetted against it, is framed by a pair of bottle-green velvet curtains, pulled back.

And does it begin now?—but this Cox is a cool number. He doesn't come on with the street epithets and interjections and the rest of the rhetoric and red eyes used for mau-mauing the white liberals, as it is called.

"The Black Panther Party," he starts off, "stands for a ten-point program that was handed down in October 1966 by our Minister of Defense, Huey P. Newton . . ." and he starts going through the ten points . . . "We want an educational system that expresses the true nature of this decadent society" . . . "We want all black men exempt from military service" . . . "We want all black men who are in jail to be set free. We want them to be set free because they have not had fair trials. We've been tried by predominantly middle-class, all-white juries" . . . "And most important of all, we want peace . . . see . . . We want peace, but there can be no peace as long as a society is racist and one part of society engages in systematic oppression of another" . . . "We want a plebiscite by the United Nations to be held in black communities, so that we can control our own destiny" . . .

Everyone in the room, of course, is drinking in his performance like tiger's milk, for the . . . Soul, as it were. All love the tone of his voice, which is Confidential Hip. And yet his delivery falls into strangely formal patterns. What are these block phrases, such as "our Minister of Defense, Huey P. Newton"—

"Some people think that we are racist, because the news media find it useful to create that impression in order to support the power structure, which we have nothing to do with . . . see . . . They like for the Black Panther Party to be made to look like a racist organization, because that camouflages the true class nature of the struggle. But they find it harder and harder to keep up that camouflage and are driven to campaigns of harassment and violence to try to eliminate the Black Panther Party. Here in New York twenty-one members of the Black Panther Party were indicted last April on ridiculous charges of conspiring to blow up department stores and flower gardens. They've had twenty-seven bail hearings since last April . . . see . . ."

—But everyone in here loves the *sees* and the *you knows*. They are so, somehow . . . *black* . . . so *funky* . . . so metrical . . . Without ever bringing it fully into consciousness everyone responds—communes over—the fact that he uses them not for emphasis but for punctuation, metrically, much like the *uhs* favored by High Church Episcopal ministers, as in, "And bless, uh, these gifts, uh, to Thy use and us to, uh, Thy service"—

". . . they've had twenty-seven bail hearings since last April . . . see . . . and every time the judge has refused to lower the bail from $100,000 . . . Yet a group of whites accused of actually bombing buildings—they were able to get bail. So that clearly demonstrates the racist nature of the campaign against the Black Panther Party. We don't say 'bail' any more, we say 'ransom,' for such repressive bail can only be called ransom.

"The situation here in New York is very explosive, as you can see, with people stacked up on top of each other. They can hardly deal with them when they're *un*organized, so that when a group comes along like the Black Panthers, they want to eliminate that group by any means . . . see . . . and so that stand has been embraced by J. Edgar Hoover, who feels that we are the greatest threat to the power structure. They try to create the impression that we are engaged in criminal activities. What are these 'criminal activities'? We have instituted a breakfast program, to address ourselves to the needs of the community. We feed hungry children every morning before they go to school. So far this program is on a small scale. We're only feeding fifty thousand children nationwide, but the only money we have for this program is donations from the merchants in the neighborhoods. We have a program to establish clinics in the black communities and in other ways also we are addressing ourselves to the needs of the community . . . see . . . So the people know the power structure is lying when they say we are engaged in criminal activities. So the pigs are driven to desperate acts, like the murder of our deputy chairman, Fred Hampton, in his bed . . . see . . . in his sleep . . . But when they got desperate and took off their camouflage and murdered Fred Hampton, in his bed, in his sleep, see, that kind of shook people up, because they saw the tactics of the power structure for what they were. . . .

"We relate to a phrase coined by Malcolm X: 'By any means necessary' . . . you see . . . 'By any means necessary' . . . and by that we mean that we recognize that if you're attacked, you have the right to defend yourself. The pigs, they say the Black Panthers are armed, the Black Panthers have weapons . . . see . . . and therefore they have the right to break in and murder us in our beds. I don't think there's anybody in here who wouldn't defend themselves if somebody came in and attacked them or their families . . . see . . . I don't think there's anybody in here who wouldn't defend themselves . . ."

—and every woman in the room thinks of her husband . . . with his cocoa-butter jowls and Dior Men's Boutique pajamas . . . ducking into the bathroom and locking the door and turning the shower on, so he can say later that he didn't hear a thing—

"We call them pigs, and rightly so," says Don Cox, "because they have the way of making the victim look like the criminal, and the criminal look like the victim. So every Panther must be ready to defend himself. That was handed down by our Minister of Defense, Huey P. Newton: Everybody who does not have the means to defend himself in his home, or if he does have the means and he does not defend himself—we expel *that man* . . . see . . . As our Minister of Defense, Huey P. Newton, says, 'Any unarmed people are slaves, or are slaves in the real meaning of the word' . . . We recognize that this country is the most oppressive country in the world, maybe in the history of the world. The pigs have the weapons and they are ready to use them on the people, and we recognize this as being very bad. They are ready to commit genocide against those who stand up against them, and we recognize this as being very bad.

"All we want is the good life, the same as you. To live in peace and lead the good life, that's all we want . . . see . . . But right now there's no way we can do that. I want to read something to you:

" 'When in the course of human events, it becomes necessary for one people to dissolve the political bands which have connected them with another, and . . .' " He reads straight through it, every word. " '. . . and, accordingly, all experience hath shown, that mankind are more disposed to suffer, while evils are sufferable, than to right themselves by abolishing the forms to which they are accustomed. But when a long train of abuses and usurpations, pursuing invariably the same object, evinces a design to reduce them under absolute despotism, it is their right, it is their duty, to throw off such government, and to provide new guards for their future security.'

"You know what that's from?"—and he looks out at everyone and hesitates before laying this gasper on them—"That's from the Declaration of Independence, the American Declaration of Independence. And we will defend ourselves and do like it says . . . you know? . . . and that's about it."

The "that's about it" part seems so casual, so funky, so right, after the rhetoric of what he has been saying. And then he sits down and sinks out of sight behind one of the grand pianos.

The thing is beginning to move. And—hell, yes, the *Reichstag fire*! Another man gets up, a white named Gerald Lefcourt, who is chief counsel for the Panther 21, a young man with thick black hair and the muttonchops of the Movement and that great motor inside of him that young courtroom lawyers ought to have. He lays the Reichstag fire on them. He reviews the Panther case and then he says:

"I believe that this odious situation could be compared to

the Reichstag fire attempt"—he's talking about the way the Nazis used the burning of the Reichstag as the pretext for first turning loose the Gestapo and exterminating all political opposition in Germany—"and I believe that this trial could also be compared to the Reichstag trial . . . in many ways . . . and that opened an era that this country could be heading for. That could be the outcome of this case, an era of the Right, and the only thing that can stop it is for people like ourselves to make a noise and make a noise now."

. . . and not be Krupps, Junkers, or Good Germans . . .

". . . We had an opportunity to question the Grand Jury, and we found out some interesting things. They all have net worths averaging $300,000, and they all come from this neighborhood," says Lefcourt, nodding as if to take in the whole Upper East Side. And suddenly everyone feels, really *feels,* that there are two breeds of mankind in the great co-ops of Park Avenue, the blue-jowled rep-tied Brook Club Junker reactionaries in the surrounding buildings . . . and the few *attuned* souls here in Lenny's penthouse. ". . . They all have annual incomes in the area of $35,000 . . . And you're supposed to have a 'jury of your peers' . . . They were shocked at the questions we were asking them. They shouldn't have to answer such questions, that was the idea. They all belong to the Grand Jury Association. They're somewhat like a club. They have lunch together once in a while. A lot of them went to school together. They have no more understanding of the Black Panthers than President Nixon."

The Junkers! Leon Quat says: "Fascism always begins by persecuting the least powerful and least popular movement. It will be the Panthers today, the students tomorrow—and then . . . the Jews and other troublesome minorities! . . . What price civil liberties! . . . Now let's start this off with the gifts in four figures. Who is ready to make a contribution of a thousand dollars or more?"

All at once—nothing. But the little gray man sitting next to Felicia, the gray man with the sideburns, pops up and hands a piece of paper to Quat and says: "Mr. Clarence Jones asked me to say—he couldn't be here, but he's contributing $7,500 to the defense fund!"

"Oh! That's marvelous!" says Felicia.

Then the voice of Lenny from the back of the room: "As a guest of my wife"—he smiles—"I'll give my fee for the next performance of *Cavalleria Rusticana*." Comradely laughter. Applause. "I *hope* that will be four figures!"

Things are moving again. Otto Preminger speaks up from the sofa down front: "I geeve a t'ousand dollars!"

Right on. Quat says: "I can't assure you that it's tax deductible." He smiles. "I wish I could, but I can't." Well, the man looks brighter and brighter every minute. He knows a Radical Chic audience when he sees one. Those words are magic in the age of Radical Chic: it's *not* tax deductible.

The contributions start coming faster, only $250 or $300 at a clip, but faster . . . Sheldon Harnick . . . Bernie and Hilda Fishman . . . Judith Bernstein . . . Mr. and Mrs. Burton Lane . . .

"I know some of you are caught with your Dow-Jones averages down," says Quat, "but come on—"

Quat says: "We have a $300 contribution from Harry Belafonte!"

"No, no," says Julie Belafonte.

"I'm sorry," says Quat, "it's Julie's private money! I apologize. After all, there's a women's liberation movement sweeping the country, and I want this marked down as a gift from *Mrs.* Belafonte!" Then he says: "I know you want to get to the question period, but I know there's more gold in this mine. I think we've reached the point where we can pass out the blank checks."

More contributions . . . $100 from Mrs. August Heckscher . . .

"We'll take *any*thing!" says Quat. "We'll take it all!" . . . He's high on the momentum of his fundraiser voice . . . "You'll leave here with nothing!"

But finally he wraps it up. A beautiful ash-blond girl with the most perfect Miss Porter's face speaks up. She's wearing a leather and tweed dress. She looks like a Junior Leaguer graduating to the Ungaro Boutique.

"I'd like to ask Mr. Cox a question," she says. Cox is standing up again, by the grand piano. "Besides the breakfast program," she says, "do you have any other community programs, and what are they like?"

Cox starts to tell about a Black Panther program to set up medical clinics in the ghettos, and so on, but soon he is talking about a Panther demand that police be required to live in the community they patrol. "If you police the community, you must live there . . . see . . . Because if he lives in the community, he's going to think twice before he brutalizes us, because we can deal with him when he comes home at night . . . see . . . We are also working to start liberation schools for black children, and these liberation schools will actually teach them about their environment, because the way they are now taught, they are taught not to see their real environment . . . see . . . They get Donald Duck and Mother Goose and all that lame happy jive . . . you know . . . We'd like to take kids on tours of the white suburbs, like Scarsdale, and like that, and let them see how their oppressors live . . . you know . . . but so far we don't have the money to carry out these programs to meet the real needs of the community. The only money we have is what we get from the merchants in the black community when we ask them for donations, which they *should give,* because they are the exploiters of the black community"—

—and *shee-ut.* What the hell is Cox getting into that for? Quat and the little gray man are ready to spring in at any lonesome split second. For God's sake, Cox, don't open that can of worms. Even in this bunch of upholstered skulls there are people who can figure out just *who* those merchants are, what group, and just how they are *asked* for donations, and we've been free of that little issue all evening, man—don't bring out *that* ball-breaker—

But the moment is saved. Suddenly there is a much more urgent question from the rear: "Who do you call to give a party? Who do you call to give a party?"

Every head spins around . . . Quite a sight . . . It's a slender blond man who has pushed his way up to the front ranks of the standees. He's wearing a tuxedo. He's wearing black-frame glasses and his blond hair is combed back straight in the Eaton Square manner. He looks like the intense Yale man from out of one of those 1927 Frigidaire ads in *The Saturday Evening Post,* when the way to sell anything was to show Harry Yale in the background, in a tuxedo, with his pageboy-bobbed young lovely, heading off to dinner at the New Haven Lawn Club. The man still has his hand up in the air like the star student of the junior class.

"I won't be able to stay for everything you have to say," he says, "but who do you call to give a party?"

In fact, it is Richard Feigen, owner of the Feigen Gallery, 79th near Madison. He arrived on the art scene and the social scene from Chicago three years ago . . . He's been moving up hand over hand ever since . . . like a champion . . . Tonight—the tuxedo—tonight there is a reception at the Museum of Modern Art . . . right on . . . a "contributing members'" reception, a private viewing not open to mere "members" . . . But before the museum reception itself, which is at 8:30, there are private dinners . . . right? . . . which are the *real* openings . . . in the homes of great collectors or great climbers or the old Protestant elite, marvelous dinner parties, the real thing, black tie, and these dinners are the only true certification of where one stands in this whole realm of Art & Society . . . The whole game depends on whose home one is invited to before the opening . . . And the game ends as the host gathers everyone up about 8:45 for the trek to the museum itself, and the guests say, almost ritually, "God! I wish we could see the show from here! It's too delightful! I simply don't want to *move*!" . . . And, of course, they mean it! Absolutely! For them, the opening is already over, the hand is played . . . And Richard Feigen, man of the hour, replica 1927 Yale man, black tie and Eaton Square hair, has dropped in, on the way, *en passant,* to the Bernsteins', to take in the other end of the Culture tandem, Radical Chic . . . and the rightness of it, the exhilaration, seems to sweep through him, and he thrusts his hand into the air, and somehow Radical Chic reaches its highest, purest state in that moment . . . as Richard Feigen, in his tuxedo, breaks in to ask, from the bottom of his heart, "Who do you call to give a party?"

.   .   .

THERE YOU HAD A TREND, A FASHION, IN ITS MOMENT OF naked triumph. How extraordinary that just thirty minutes later Radical Chic would be—

But at that moment Radical Chic was the new wave supreme in New York Society. It had been building for more than six months. It had already reached the fashion pages of *Vogue* and was moving into the food column. *Vogue* was already preparing a column entitled "Soul Food."

"The cult of Soul Food," it began, "is a form of Black self-awareness and, to a lesser degree, of white sympathy for the Black drive to self-reliance. It is as if those who ate the beans and greens of necessity in the cabin doorways were brought into communion with those who, not having to, eat those foods voluntarily as a sacrament. The present struggle is emphasized in the act of breaking traditional bread . . .

Sweet Potato Pone

  3 CUPS FINELY GRATED RAW SWEET POTATOES

  1/2 CUP SWEET MILK

  2 TABLESPOONS MELTED BUTTER

  1/2 TEASPOON EACH:

    CINNAMON, GINGER, POWDERED CLOVES AND NUTMEG

  2 EGGS

  SALT

  1/2 CUP BROWN SUGAR

  1/2 CUP MOLASSES OR HONEY

"Mix together potatoes, milk, melted butter, cinnamon, ginger, powdered cloves, nutmeg, and eggs. Add a pinch of salt, brown sugar, and the molasses or honey. (Molasses gives the authentic pone; honey a dandified version.)"

A little sacramental pone . . . as the young'uns skitter back in through the loblolly-pine cabin doorway to help Mama put the cinnamon, ginger, powdered cloves, and nutmeg back on the Leslie Foods "Spice Island" spice rack . . . and thereby finish up the communion with those who, not having to, eat those foods voluntarily as a sacrament.

Very nice! In fact, this sort of *nostalgie de la boue,* or romanticizing of primitive souls, was one of the things that brought Radical Chic to the fore in New York Society. *Nostalgie de la boue* is a nineteenth-century French term that means, literally, "nostalgia for the mud." Within New York Society *nostalgie de la boue* was a great motif throughout the 1960's, from the moment two socialites, Susan Stein and Christina Paolozzi, discovered the Peppermint Lounge and the twist and two of the era's first pet primitives, Joey Dee and Killer Joe Piro. *Nostalgie de la boue* tends to be a favorite motif whenever a great many new faces and a lot of new money enter Society. New arrivals have always had two ways of certifying their superiority over the hated "middle class." They can take on the trappings of aristocracy, such as grand architecture, servants, parterre boxes, and high protocol; and they can indulge in the gauche thrill of taking on certain styles of the lower orders. The two are by no means mutually exclusive; in fact, they are always used in combination. In England during the Regency period, *nostalgie de la boue* was very much the rage. London socialites during the Regency adopted the flamboyant capes and wild driving styles of the coach drivers, the "bruiser" fashions and hair styles of the bare-knuckle prize fighters, the see-through, jutting-nipple fashions of the tavern girls, as well as a reckless new dance, the waltz. Such affectations were meant to convey the arrogant self-confidence of the aristocrat as opposed to the middle-class striver's obsession with propriety and keeping up appearances. During the 1960's in New York *nostalgie de la boue* took the form of the vogue of rock music, the twist-frug genre of dances, Pop Art, Camp, the courting of pet primitives such as the Rolling Stones and José Torres, and innumerable dress fashions summed up in the recurrent image of the wealthy young man with his turtleneck jersey meeting his muttonchops at mid-jowl, à la the 1962 Sixth Avenue Automat bohemian, bidding good night to an aging doorman dressed in the mode of an 1870 Austrian army colonel.

At the same time Society in New York was going through another of those new-money upheavals that have made the social history of New York read like the political history of the Caribbean; which is to say, a revolution every twenty years, if not sooner. Aristocracies, in the European sense, are always based upon large hereditary landholdings. Early in the history of the United States, Jefferson's crusade against primogeniture eliminated the possibility of a caste of hereditary land barons. The great landholders, such as the Carrolls, Livingstons, and Schuylers, were soon upstaged by the federal bankers, such as the Biddles and Lenoxes. There followed wave after wave of new plutocrats with new sources of wealth: the international bankers, the real-estate speculators, the Civil War profiteers, railroad magnates, Wall Street operators, oil and steel trust manipulators, and so on. By the end of the Civil War, social life in New York was already The Great Barbecue, to borrow a term from Vernon L. Parrington, the literary historian. During the season of 1865–66 there were six hundred Society balls given in New York, and a great wall of brownstone mansions went up along Fifth Avenue.

In the early 1880's New York's social parvenus—the people

who were the Sculls, Paleys, Engelhards, Holzers, of their day—were the Vanderbilts, Rockefellers, Huntingtons, and Goulds. They built the Metropolitan Opera House for the simple reason that New York's prevailing temple of Culture, the Academy of Music, built just twenty-nine years before at 14th Street and Irving Place, had only eighteen fashionable proscenium boxes, and they were monopolized by families like the Lorillards, Traverses, Belmonts, Stebbinses, Gandys, and Barlows. The status of the Goulds and Vanderbilts was revealed in the sort of press coverage the Met's opening (October 22, 1883) received: "The Goulds and the Vanderbilts and people of that ilk perfumed the air with the odor of crisp greenbacks."

By the 1960's yet another new industry had begun to dominate New York life, namely, communications—the media. At the same time the erstwhile "minorities" of the first quarter of the century had begun to come into their own. Jews, especially, but also many Catholics, were eminent in the media and in Culture. So, by 1965—as in 1935, as in 1926, as in 1883, as in 1866, as in 1820—New York had two Societies, "Old New York" and "New Society." In every era, "Old New York" has taken a horrified look at "New Society" and expressed the devout conviction that a genuine aristocracy, good blood, good bone—themselves—was being defiled by a horde of rank climbers. This has been an all-time favorite number. In the 1960's this quaint belief was magnified by the fact that many members of "New Society," for the first time, were not Protestant. The names and addresses of "Old New York" were to be found in the Social Register, which even ten years ago was still confidently spoken of as the Stud Book and the Good Book. It was, and still is, almost exclusively a roster of Protestant families. Today, however, the Social Register's annual shuffle, in which errant socialites, e.g., John Jacob Astor, are dropped from the Good Book, hardly even rates a yawn. The fact is that "Old New York"—except for those members who also figure in "New Society," e.g., Nelson Rockefeller, John Hay Whitney, Mrs. Wyatt Cooper—is no longer good copy, and without publicity it has *never* been easy to rank as a fashionable person in New York City.

The press in New York has tended to favor New Society in every period, and to take it seriously, if only because it provides "news." For example, the $400,000 Bradley Martin ball of 1897. The John Bradley Martins were late-comers from Troy, New York, who had inserted an invisible hyphen between the Bradley and the Martin and preferred to be known as the Bradley Martins, after the manner of the Gordon Walkers in England. For the record, the Bradley Martins staged their own ball in 1897 as "an impetus to trade" to alleviate the suffering of the poor. Inflamed by the grandeur of it all, the newspapers described the affair down to the last piece of Mechlin lace and the last drop of seed pearl. It was the greatest single one-shot social climb in New York history prior to Truman Capote's masked ball in 1966.

By the 1960's New York newspapers had an additional reason to favor New Society. The Seventh Avenue garment trade, the newspapers' greatest source of advertising revenue, had begun recruiting New Society in droves to promote new fashions. It got to the point where for a matron to be photographed in the front row at the spring or fall showings of European copies at Ohrbach's, by no means the most high-toned clothing store in the world, became a certification of "socialite" status second to none. But this was nothing new, either. Forty years ago firms flogging things like Hardman pianos, Pond's cold cream, Simmons metal beds, and Camel cigarettes found that matrons in the clans Harriman, Longworth, Belmont, Fish, Lowell, Iselin, and Carnegie were only too glad to switch to their products and be photographed with them in their homes, mainly for the sheer social glory of the publicity.

Another source of publicity was aid to the poor. New York's new socialites, in whatever era, have always paid their dues to "the poor," via charity, as a way of claiming the nobility inherent in *noblesse oblige* and of legitimizing their wealth. The Bradley Martin ball was a case in point. New money usually works harder in this direction than old. John D. Rockefeller, under the guidance of Ivy P. Lee, the original "public relations counsel," managed to convert his reputation from that of robber baron and widow-fleecer to that of august old sage philanthropist so rapidly that small children cried when he died. His strategy was to set up several hundred million dollars' worth of foundations for Culture and scientific research.

Among the new socialites of the 1960's, especially those from the one-time "minorities," this old social urge to do well by doing good, as it says in the song, has taken a more specific political direction. This has often been true of Jewish socialites and culturati, although it has by no means been confined to them. Politically, Jews have been unique among the groups that came to New York in the great migrations of the late nineteenth and early twentieth centuries. Many such groups, of course, were left or liberal during the first generation, but as families began to achieve wealth, success, or, simply, security, they tended to grow more and more conservative in philosophy. The Irish are a case in point. But forced by twentieth- as well as nineteenth-century history to remain on guard against right-wing movements, even wealthy and successful Jewish families have tended to remain faithful to their original liberal-left world-view. In fact, according to Seymour Martin Lipset, Nathan Glazer, and Kenneth Keniston, an unusually high proportion of campus militants come from well-to-do Jewish families. They have developed the so-called "red diaper baby" theory to explain it. According to Lipset, many Jewish children have grown up in families which "around the breakfast table, day after day, in Scarsdale, Newton, Great Neck, and Beverly Hills," have discussed racist and reactionary tendencies in American society. Lipset speaks of the wealthy Jewish family with the "right-wing life style" (e.g., a majority of Americans outside of the South who have full-time servants are Jewish, according to a study by Lipset, Glazer, and Herbert Hyman) and the "left-wing outlook."

This phenomenon is rooted in Jewish experience not only in America but in Europe as well. Anti-Semitism was an issue in the French Revolution; throughout Europe during the nineteenth century all sorts of legal and *de facto* restrictions against Jews were abolished. Yet Jews were still denied the social advantages that routinely accrued to Gentiles of comparable wealth and achievement. They were not accepted in Society, for example, and public opinion generally remained anti-Semitic. Not only out of resentment, but also for sheer self-defense, even wealthy Jews tended to support left-wing political parties. They had no choice. Most organizations on the right had an anti-Semitic or, at the very least, an all-Christian, cast to them. Jews coming to the United States in the late nineteenth and early twentieth centuries saw little to choose from among the major political parties. As to which party seemed the more anti-Jewish, the Democratic or the Republican, it was a toss-up. The Republicans had abolished slavery, but the party was full of Know-Nothings and anti-immigrant nativists. Even the Populists were anti-Jewish. For example, Tom Watson, the famous Populist senator, denounced the oil cartels, fought against American involvement in World War I as a cynical capitalist adventure, defended Eugene Debs, demanded U.S. recognition of the Soviet Union shortly after the Revolution—and was openly anti-Semitic and anti-Catholic and was laid out in the shadow of an eight-foot-high cross of roses from the Ku Klux Klan at his funeral in 1922. As a result, many Jews, especially in cities like New York and Chicago, backed the socialist parties that thrived briefly during the 1920's. In many cases Jews were the main support. At the same time Jews continued to look for some wing of the major parties that they could live with, and finally found it in the New Deal.

For years many Jewish members of New Society have supported black organizations such as the NAACP, the Urban League, and CORE. And no doubt they have been sincere about it, because these organizations have never had much social cachet; i.e., they have had "middle class" written all over them. All one had to do was look at the "Negro leaders" involved. There they were, up on the dais at the big hotel banquet, wearing their white shirts, their Hart Schaffner & Marx suits three sizes too big, and their academic solemnity. By last year, however, the picture had changed. In 1965 two new political movements, the anti-war movement and black power, began to gain great backing among culturati in New York. By 1968 the two movements began to achieve social as well as cultural prestige with the Presidential campaigns of Eugene McCarthy and Robert Kennedy; especially Kennedy's. Kennedy was not merely an anti-war candidate; he also made a point of backing Cesar Chavez's grape workers—"La Causa," "La Huelga"—in California. On the face of it, La Causa was a labor-union movement. But La Causa quickly came to symbolize the political ambitions of all lower-class Mexican-Americans—*Chicanos,* "Brown Americans"—and, by extension, that of all colored Americans, including blacks.

The black movement itself, of course, had taken on a much more electric and romantic cast. What a relief it was—socially—in New York—when the leadership seemed to shift from middle class to . . . *funky!* From A. Philip Randolph, Dr. Martin Luther King, and James Farmer . . . to Stokely, Rap, LeRoi, and Eldridge! This meant that the tricky business of the fashionable new politics could now be integrated with a tried and true social motif: *nostalgie de la boue.* The upshot was Radical Chic.

From the beginning it was pointless to argue about the sincerity of Radical Chic. Unquestionably the basic impulse, "red diaper" or otherwise, was sincere. But, as in most human endeavors focused upon an ideal, there seemed to be some double-track thinking going on. On the first track—well, one *does* have a sincere concern for the poor and the underprivileged and an honest outrage against discrimination. One's heart does cry out—quite spontaneously!—upon hearing how the police have dealt with the Panthers, dragging an epileptic like Lee Berry out of his hospital bed and throwing him into the Tombs. When one thinks of Mitchell and Agnew and Nixon and all of their Captain Beefheart Maggie & Jiggs New York Athletic Club troglodyte crypto–Horst Wessel Irish Oyster Bar Construction Worker followers, then one understands why poor blacks like the Panthers might feel driven to drastic solutions, and—well, anyway, one truly *feels* for them. One really does. On the other hand—on the second track in one's mind, that is—one also has a sincere concern for maintaining a proper East Side life-style in New York Society. And this concern is just as sincere as the first, and just as deep. It really is. It really *does* become part of one's psyche. For example, one *must* have a weekend place, in the country or by the shore, all year round preferably, but certainly from the middle of May to the middle of September. It is hard to get across to outsiders an understanding of how *absolute* such apparently trivial needs are. One *feels* them in his solar plexus. When one thinks of being trapped in New York Saturday after Saturday in July or August, doomed to be a part of those fantastically dowdy herds roaming past Bonwit's and Tiffany's at dead noon in the sandstone sun-broil, 92 degrees, daddies from Long Island in balloon-seat Bermuda shorts bought at the Times Square Store in Oceanside and fat mommies with white belled pants stretching over their lower bellies and crinkling up in the crotch like some kind of Dacron-polyester labia—well, anyway, then one truly *feels* the need to obey at least the minimal rules of New York Society. One really does.

One rule is that *nostalgie de la boue*—i.e., the styles of romantic, raw-vital, Low Rent primitives—are good; and *middle class,* whether black or white, is bad. Therefore, Radical Chic invariably favors radicals who seem primitive, exotic, and romantic, such as the grape workers, who are not merely radical and "of the soil" but also Latin; the Panthers, with their leather pieces, Afros, shades, and shoot-outs; and the Red Indians, who, of course, had always seemed primitive, exotic, and romantic. At the outset, at least, all three groups had something else to recommend them, as well: they were headquartered three thousand miles away from the East Side of Manhattan, in places like Delano (the grape workers), Oakland (the Panthers), and Arizona and New Mexico (the Indians). They weren't likely to become too much . . . *underfoot,* as it were. Exotic, Romantic, Far Off . . . as we shall soon see, other favorite creatures of Radical Chic had the same attractive qualities; namely, the ocelots, jaguars, cheetahs, and Somali leopards.

Rule no. 2 was that no matter what, one should always maintain a proper address, a proper scale of interior decoration, and servants. Servants, especially, were one of the last absolute dividing lines between those truly "in Society," New or Old, and the great scuffling mass of middle-class strivers paying up to $2,500-a-month rent or buying expensive co-ops all over the East Side. There are no two ways about it. One *must* have servants. Having servants becomes such a psychological necessity that there are many women in Society today who may be heard to complain in all honesty about how hard it is to find a nurse for the children to fill in on the regular nurse's day off. There is the famous Mrs. C——, one of New York's richest widows, who has a ten-room duplex on Sutton Place, the good part of Sutton Place as opposed to the Miami Beach–looking part, one understands, but who is somehow absolute poison with servants and can't keep anything but day help and is constantly heard to lament: "What good is all the money in the world if you can't come home at night and know there will be someone there to take your coat and fix you a drink?" There is true anguish behind that remark!

In the era of Radical Chic, then, what a collision course was set between the absolute need for servants—and the fact that the servant was the absolute symbol of what the new movements, black or brown, were struggling against! How absolutely urgent, then, became the search for the only way out: white servants!

THE FIRST BIG RADICAL CHIC PARTY, THE EPOCHAL EVENT, so to speak, was the party that Assemblyman Andrew Stein gave for the grape workers on his father's estate in Southampton on June 29, 1969. The grape workers had already been brought into New York social life. Carter and Amanda Burden, the "Moonflower Couple" of the 1960's, had given a party for them in their duplex in River House, on East 52nd Street overlooking the East River. Some of New York's best graphic artists, such as Paul Davis, had done exquisite posters for "La Causa" and "La Huelga." The grape workers had begun a national campaign urging consumers to boycott California table grapes, and nowhere was the ban more strictly observed than in Radically Chic circles. Chavez became one of the few union leaders with a romantic image.

Andrew Stein's party, then, was the epochal event, not so much because he was fashionable as because the grape workers were. The list of guests and sponsors for the event was first-rate. Henry Ford II's daughter Anne (Mrs. Giancarlo Uzielli) was chairman, and Ethel Kennedy was honorary chairman. Mrs. Kennedy was making her first public appearance since the assassination of her husband in 1968. Stein himself was the twenty-four-year-old son of Jerry Finkelstein, who had made a small fortune in public relations and built it up into a firm called Struthers Wells. Finkelstein was also a power in the New York State Democratic Party and, in fact, recently became the party's New York City chairman. His son Andrew had shortened his name from Finkelstein to Stein and was noted not only for the impressive parties he gave but for his election to the State Assembly from Manhattan's East Side. The rumor was that his father had spent $500,000 on his campaign. No one who knew state politics believed that, however, since for half that sum he could have bought enough of Albany to have the boy declared king.

The party was held on the lawn outside Finkelstein's huge *cottage orné* by the sea in Southampton. There were two signs by the main entrance to the estate. One said Finkelstein and the other said Stein. The guests came in saying the usual, which was, "You can't take the Fink out of Finkelstein." No one turned back, however. From the beginning the afternoon was full of the delicious status contradictions and incongruities that provide much of the electricity for Radical Chic. Chavez himself was not there, but a contingent of grape workers was on hand, including Chavez's first lieutenant, Andrew Imutan, and Imutan's wife and three sons. The grape workers were all in work clothes, Levi's, chinos, Sears balloon-seat twills, Kmart sports shirts, and so forth. The socialites, meanwhile, arrived at the height of the 1969 summer season of bell-bottom silk pants suits, Pucci clings, Dunhill blazers, and Turnbull & Asser neckerchiefs. A mariachi band played for the guests as they arrived. Marvelous! Everyone's status radar was now so sensitive that the mariachi band seemed like a *faux pas*. After all, mariachi bands, with those Visit Mexico costumes on and those sad trumpets that keep struggling up to the top of the note but always fall off and then try to struggle back up again, are the prime white-tourist Mexicans. At a party for La Causa, the grape workers, the fighting *Chicanos*—this was a little like bringing Ma Goldberg in to entertain the Stern Gang. But somehow it was ... *delicious* to experience such weird status thrills ...

When the fund-raising began, Andrew Imutan took a microphone up on the terrace above the lawn and asked everybody to shut their eyes and pretend they were a farm worker's wife in the dusty plains of Delano, California, eating baloney sandwiches for breakfast at 3 a.m. before heading out into the fields ... So they all stood there in their Pucci dresses, Gucci shoes, Capucci scarves, either imagining they were grape workers' wives or wondering if the goddamned wind would ever stop. The wind had come up off the ocean and it was wrecking everybody's hair. People were standing there with their hands pressed against their heads as if the place had been struck by a brain-piercing ray from the Purple Dimension. Andrew Stein's hair was long, full, and at the outset had been especially well coifed in the Roger's 58th Street French manner, and now it was ... a wreck ... He kept one hand on his head the whole time, like the boy at the dike ... "eating baloney sandwiches for breakfast at 3 a.m. ...."

Then Frank Mankiewicz, who had been Robert Kennedy's press secretary, got up and said, "Well, all I know is, if we can only raise twenty percent of the money that has gone into all the Puccis I see here today, we'll be doing all right!" He waited for the laughter, and all he got was the ocean breeze in his face. By then everyone present was thinking approximately the same thing ... and it was *delicious* in that weird way ... but to just blurt it out was a strange sort of counter-gaffe.

Nevertheless, Radical Chic had arrived. The fall social season of 1969 was a big time for it. People like Jean vanden Heuvel gave parties for *Ramparts* magazine, which had by now become completely a magazine of the barricades, and for the Chicago Eight. Jules Feiffer gave a party for the G.I. coffee houses, at which Richard Avedon, America's most famous fashion photographer, took portraits of everybody who made a $25 contribution to the cause. He had his camera and lights set up in the dining room. As a matter of fact, Avedon had become a kind of court photographer to the Movement. He was making his pentennial emergence to see where it was now at. Five years before he had emerged from his studio to take a look around and had photographed and edited an entire issue of *Harper's Bazaar* to record his findings, which were of the Pop, Op, Rock, Andy, Rudi, and Go-Go variety. Now Avedon was putting together a book about the Movement. He went to Chicago for the trial of The Eight and set up a studio in a hotel near the courthouse to do portraits of the celebrities and activists who testified at the trial or watched it or circled around it in one way or another.

Meanwhile, some of the most prestigious young matrons in San Francisco and New York were into an organization called Friends of the Earth. Friends of the Earth was devoted to the proposition that women should not buy coats or other apparel made from the hides of such dying species as leopards, cheetahs, jaguars, ocelots, tigers, Spanish lynx, Asiatic lions, red wolves, sea otter, giant otter, polar bear, mountain zebra, alligators, crocodiles, sea turtles, vicuñas, timber wolves, wolverines, margays, kolinskies, martens, fishers, fitch, sables, servals, and mountain lions. On the face of it, there was nothing very radical about this small gesture in the direction of conservation, or ecology, as it is now known. Yet Friends of the Earth was Radical Chic, all right. The radical part began with the simple fact that the movement was not tax deductible. Friends of the Earth is an offshoot of the Sierra Club. The Sierra Club's preeminence in the conservation movement began at precisely the moment when the federal government declared it a political organization, chiefly due to its fight against proposed dam projects in the Grand Canyon. That meant that contributions to it were no longer tax deductible. One of the Sierra Club's backstage masterminds, the late Howard Gossage, used to tell David Brower, the Sierra Club's president: "That's the grea-a-a-atest thing that ever happened to you. It removed all the guilt! Now the money's just rolllllllll-ing in." Then he would go into his cosmic laugh. He had an incredible cosmic laugh, Gossage did. It started way back in his throat and came rolllling out, as if from Lane 27 of the Heavenly bowling alley.

No tax deduction! That became part of the canon of Radical Chic. Lay it on the line! Matrons soliciting funds for Friends of the Earth and other organizations took to making telephone calls that ended with: "All right, now, I'll expect to see your check in the mail—and it's *not* tax deductible." That was a challenge, the unspoken part of which was: You can be a tax-deductible Heart Funder, April in Paris Baller, Day Care Center-of-the-roader, if that's all you want out of your jiveass life . . . As for themselves, the Friends of the Earth actually took to the streets, picketing stores and ragging women who walked down the street with their new Somali leopard coats on. A woman's only acceptable defense was to say she had shot the animal and eaten it. The Friends of the Earth movement was not only a fight in behalf of the poor beasts but a fight against greed, against the spirit of capitalistic marauding, to call it by its right name . . . although the fight took some weird skews here and there, as Radical Chic is apt to do.

Those goddamned permutations in taste! In New York, for example, Freddy Plimpton had Jacques Kaplan, the number-one Society furrier, make her a skirt of alley-cat pelts—at least that was the way it first came out in *The New York Times*. Not for nothing is Jacques Kaplan the number-one Society furrier. He must have seen Radical Chic coming a mile away. Early in the game he himself, a furrier, started pitching in for the embattled ocelots, margays, fitch and company like there was no tomorrow. Anyway, the *Times* ran a story saying he had made a skirt of alley-cat hides for Freddy Plimpton. The idea was that alley cats, unlike ocelots and so on, are an absolute glut in the ecology and end up in the ASPCA gas chambers anyway. Supposedly it was logical to Kaplan and logical to Mrs. Plimpton—but to hundreds of little-old-lady cat lovers in Dickerson Archlock shoes, there was some kind of a weird class warp going on here . . . Slaughter the lowly alley cat to save the high-toned ocelot . . . That was the way it came out . . . and the less said about retrieving decorative hides from the gas chambers, the better. . . . They were going to picket Jacques Kaplan and raise hell about the slaughter of the alley cats. The fact that the skirt was actually made of the hides of genets, a European nuisance animal like the ferret—as the *Times* noted in a correction two days later—this was not a distinction that cut much ice with the cat lovers by that time. Slaughter the lowly alley genet to save the high-toned ocelot . . .

Other charitable organizations began to steer in the direction of Radical Chic, even if they did not go all the way and give up their tax-deductible status. For example, the gala for the University of the Streets on January 22, 1970. The University of the Streets was dedicated to "educating the 'uneducatables' of the ghetto." The gala was a dance with avant-garde music, light shows, movies, sculpture, and "multi-sensory environments." The invitation said, "Price: $125 Per Couple (Tax Deductible)" and "Dress: Beautiful." This was nothing new. What was new was that the ball would not be within the grand coving-and-pilaster insulation of a midtown hotel but down on the Lower East Side, East Seventh Street and Avenue A, at Tompkins Square, in the heart of Radically Chic Puerto Rican & black & hippie territory. The invitations came in a clear plastic box with a lid, and each had the radiant eye of a real peacock feather inside; also a flower blossom, which arrived dried up and shriveled, and many wondered, wildly, if it were some exotic Southwestern psychedelic, to be smoked. One matron on the invitation list gave the peacock feather to her daughter to take to her school, one of the city's most fashionable private grammar schools, for her class's morning game of "Show and Tell," in which some unusual object is presented, wondered over, and then explained. When she returned home, her mother asked her how the feather had gone down, whereupon the little girl burst into tears. Seven other children in her class had also brought the radiant eye of a peacock feather that morning for "Show and Tell."

Soon—just a few weeks after his first big Radical Chic party—Andrew Stein was throwing another one, this time for Bernadette Devlin, the Irish Joan of Arc. Not to be outdone, Carter Burden, his chief rival, developed what can only be termed the first Total Radical Chic life-style. In 1965 Burden, then twenty-three, and his wife Amanda, then twenty, had been singled out by *Vogue* as New York's perfect young married couple. They had moved into an ample co-op in the Dakota and had coated and encrusted it with a layer of antiques that was like the final triumph of a dowager duchess in an Angela Thirkell novel. They were described as possessing not merely wealth, however, but also "enquiring minds." To clinch the point, *Vogue* pointed out that "Mrs. Burden, with the help of a maid, is learning how to keep house." Just a year after their Dakota triumph, the Burdens moved to River House, flagship of the East River co-op gold coast from Beekman Place to Sutton Place. They set up house in a duplex and hired Parish-Hadley, interior decorators to Jacqueline Kennedy, Jay and Sharon Rockefeller, the Paleys, the Wrightsmans, and the Engelhards. "Gossip has it," said *Town & Country,* "that a cool million was invested in Carter and Amanda Burden's River House apartment alone, just for backgrounds. Most of the art and furniture were already there." But in a couple of years the Burdens went Radical Chic. True, they did not give up their River House showplace. In fact, they did not disturb or deplete its treasures in the slightest. But they did set up another apartment on Fifth Avenue at 100th Street. This established residence for Burden in the Fourth Councilmanic District and qualified him to run for the New York City Council; successfully, as it turned out. It also gave him the most exquisitely poised Total Radical Chic apartment in New York.

There was genius to the way the Burdens gave visual expression to the double-track mental atmosphere of Radical Chic. The building is perhaps the scruffiest co-op building on Upper Fifth Avenue. The paint job in the lobby and hallways looks like a 1947 destroyer's. There is a doorman but no elevator man; one has to take himself up in an old West Side–style Serge Automatic elevator. But . . . it *is* a co-op and it *is* on Upper Fifth Avenue. The apartment itself has low ceilings, a small living room, and only five rooms in all. But it *does* overlook Central Park. It is furnished almost entirely in the sort of whimsical horrors—japanned chairs, brass beds, and so on—that end up in the attic in the country, the sort of legacies from God knows where that one never gets around to throwing away ... And yet they *are* ... amusing. The walls are covered in end-of-the-bolt paintings by fashionable artists of the decorative mode, such as Stella and Lichtenstein ... the sort of mistakes every collector makes and wonders where he will ever hang ... and yet they *are* Stellas and Lichtensteins ... somehow Burden even managed to transform himself from the Deke House chubbiness of his Early *Vogue* Period to the look known as Starved to Near Perfection. It is within this artfully balanced style of life that the Burdens have been able to groove, as they say, with the Young Lords and other pet primitives from Harlem and Spanish Harlem and at the same time fit into all the old mainline events such as the Metropolitan Museum of Art's 100th anniversary gala and be photographed doing the new boogaloo.

So ... Radical Chic was already in full swing by the time the Black Panther Party began a national fund-raising campaign late in 1969. The Panthers' organizers, like the grape workers', counted on the "cause party"—to use a term for it that was current thirty-five years ago—not merely in order to raise money. The Panthers' status was quite confused in the minds of many liberals, and to have the Panthers feted in the homes of a series of social and cultural leaders could make an important difference. Ideally, it would work out well for the socialites and culturati, too, for if there was ever a group that embodied the romance and excitement of which Radical Chic is made, it was the Panthers.

Even before the Bernsteins' party for the Panthers, there

had been at least three others, at the homes of John Simon of Random House, on Hudson Street; Richard Baron, the publisher, in Chappaqua; and Sidney and Gail Lumet, in their townhouse at Lexington Avenue and 91st Street. It was the Lumets' party that led directly to the Bernsteins'. A veteran cause organizer named Hannah Weinstein had called up Gail Lumet. She said that Murray Kempton had asked her to try to organize a party for the Black Panthers to raise money for the defense of the Panther 21.

The party was a curious one, even by the standards of Radical Chic. Many of the guests appeared not to be particularly "social" . . . more like Mr. and Mrs. Wealthy Dentist from New Rochelle. Yet there was a certain social wattage in the presence of people like Murray Kempton, Peter Stone, writer of *1776,* the Lumets themselves, and several Park Avenue matrons, the most notable being Leonard Bernstein's wife, Felicia.

Anyway, the white guests and a few academic-looking blacks were packed, sitting and standing, into the living room. Then a contingent of twelve or thirteen Black Panthers arrived. The Panthers had no choice but to assemble in the dining room and stand up—in their leather pieces, Afros, and shades—facing the whites in the living room. As a result, whenever anyone got up in the living room to speak, the audience was looking not only at the speaker but into the faces of a hard front line of Black Panthers in the dining room. Quite a tableau it was. It was at this point that a Park Avenue matron first articulated the great recurrent emotion of Radical Chic: "These are no civil-rights *Negroes* wearing gray suits three sizes too big—these are *real men!*"

The first half of the session generated the Radical Chic

emotion in its purest and most penetrating form. Not only was there the electrifying spectacle of the massed Panthers, but Mrs. Lee Berry rose and delivered a moving account of how her husband had been seized by police in his hospital room and removed summarily to jail. To tell the truth, some of the matrons were disappointed when she first opened her mouth. She had such a small, quiet voice. "I am a Panther wife," she said. *I am a Panther wife?* But her story *was* moving. Felicia Bernstein had been present up to this point and, as a long-time supporter of civil liberties, had been quite upset by what she had heard. But she had had to leave before the session was over. Each guest, as he left, was presented with a sheet of paper and asked to do one of three things: pledge a contribution to the defense fund, lend his name to an advertisement that was to appear in *The New York Times,* or make his home available for another party and fund-raising event. By the time she left, Felicia was quite ready to open her doors.

The emotional momentum was building rapidly when Ray "Masai" Hewitt, the Panthers' Minister of Education and member of the Central Committee, rose to speak. Hewitt was an intense, powerful young man and in no mood to play the diplomacy game. Some of you here, he said, may have some feelings left for the Establishment, but we don't. We want to see it die. We're Maoist revolutionaries, and we have no choice but to fight to the finish. For about thirty minutes Masai Hewitt laid it on the line. He referred now and again to "that motherfucker Nixon" and to how the struggle would not be easy, and that if buildings were burned and other violence ensued, that was only part of the struggle that the power structure had forced the oppressed minorities into. Hewitt's words tended to provoke an all-or-nothing reaction. A few who remembered the struggles of the Depression were profoundly moved, fired up with a kind of *nostalgie de that old-time religion*. But more than one Park Avenue matron was thrown into a Radical Chic confusion. The most memorable quote was: "He's a magnificent man, but suppose some simple-minded schmucks take all that business about burning down buildings *seriously?*"

Murray Kempton cooled things down a bit. He stood up and, in his professorial way, in the tweedy tones of the lecturer who clicks his pipe against his teeth like a mental metronome, he summed up the matter. Dependable old Murray put it all in the more comfortable terms of Reason Devout, after the manner of a lead piece in the periodicals he worshipped, *The New Statesman* and *The Spectator*. Murray, it turned out, was writing a book on the Panthers and otherwise doing his best for the cause. Yes, Masai Hewitt may have set the message down too hard, but that was of little consequence. In no time at all another party for the Panthers had been arranged. And this time in the home of one of the most famous men in the United States, Leonard Bernstein.

"WHO DO YOU CALL TO GIVE A PARTY!" SAYS RICHARD Feigen. "Who do you call to give a party!"

And all at once the candid voice of Radical Chic, just ringing out like that, seems about to drop Don Cox, Field Marshal of the Black Panthers, in his tracks, by Lenny's grand piano. He just stares at Feigen . . . this Yale-style blond in a tuxedo . . . And from that moment on, the evening begins to take on a weird reversal. Rather than Cox being in the role of the black militant mau-mauing the rich white liberals, he is slowly backed into a weird corner. Afro, goatee, turtleneck, and all, *he* has to be the diplomat . . . *He* has to play that all-time-loser role of the house guest trying to deal with a bunch of leaping, prancing, palsied happy-slobber Saint Bernards . . . It's a ball-breaker . . . And no wonder. For what man in all history has ever before come face to face with naked white Radical Chic running ecstatically through a Park Avenue duplex and letting it all hang out?

One of the members of the Panther defense committee, a white, manages to come up with a phone number, "691–8787," but Feigen is already pressing on:

"There is one candidate for governor," he says—quite an impressive voice—"who feels very deeply about what is going on here. He had hoped to be here tonight, but unfortunately he was detained upstate. And that's Howard Samuels. Now, what I want to know is, if he were willing to come before you and present his program, would you be willing to consider supporting it? In other words, are the Black Panthers interested in getting any political leverage within the System?"

Cox stares at him again. "Well," he says—and it is the first time he falls into that old hesitant thing of beginning a sentence with *well*—"any politician who is willing to relate to our ten-point program, we will support him actively, but we have no use for the traditional political—"

"But would you be willing to listen to such a candidate?" says Feigen.

"—the traditional political arena, because if you try to oppose the system from within the traditional political arena, you're wasting your time. Look at Powell. As soon as he began to speak for the people, they threw him out. We have no power within the system, and we will never have any power within the system. The only power we have is the power to destroy, the power to disrupt. If black people are armed with knowledge—"

"But would you be willing to listen to such a candidate?" says Feigen.

"Well," says Cox, a bit wearily, "we would refer him to our Central Committee, and if he was willing to support our ten-point program, then we would support that man."

Feigen muses sagely inside of his tuxedo. *Dapper.* A dapper dude in pinstripe suit and pencil mustache in the rear of the room, a black named Rick Haynes, president of Management Formation Inc., an organization promoting black capitalism, asks about the arrest the other night of Robert Bay and another Panther named Jolly.

"Right on," says Cox, softly, raising his left fist a bit, but only as a fraternal gesture—and through every white cortex rushes the flash about how the world here is divided between those who rate that acknowledgment—*right on*—and those who don't . . . Right on . . . Cox asks Robert Bay to stand, and his powerful form and his ferocious Afro rise from out of the midst of the people in the rows of chairs in the center of the room, he nods briefly toward Haynes and smiles and says "Right on"—there it is—and then he sits down. And Cox tells how the three detectives rousted and hassled Bay and Jolly and another man, and then the detectives went on radio station WINS and "lied about it all day." And Lefcourt gets up and tells how this has become a pattern, the cops incessantly harassing the Panthers, wherever they may be, everything from stopping them for doing 52 in a 50-mile-an-hour zone to killing Fred Hampton in his bed.

The beautiful ash-blond girl speaks up: "People like myself who feel that up to now the Panthers have been very badly treated—we don't know what to do. I mean, if you don't have money and you don't have influence, what can you do? What other community programs are there? We want to do something, but what can we do? Is there some kind of committee, or some kind of . . . I don't know . . ."

Well, baby, if you really—but Cox tells her that one of the big problems is finding churches in the black community that will help the Panthers in their breakfast program for ghetto children, and maybe people like her could help the Panthers approach the churches. "It's basically the churches who have the large kitchens that we need," he says, "but when we come to them to use their kitchens, to feed hot breakfasts to hungry children, they close the door in our faces. That's where the churches in the black community are at."

"Tell why!" says Leonard Bernstein. Hardly anybody has noticed it up to now, but Leonard Bernstein has moved from the back of the room to an easy chair up front. He's only a couple of feet from Cox. But Cox is standing up, by the piano, and Lenny is sunk down to his hip sockets in the easy chair . . . They really don't know what they're in for. Lenny is on the move. As more than one person in this room knows, Lenny treasures "the art of conversation." He treasures it, monopolizes it, conglomerates it, like a Jay Gould, an Onassis, a Cornfeld of Conversation. Anyone who has spent a three-day weekend with Lenny in the country, by the shore, or captive on some lonesome cay in the Windward Islands knows that feeling—the alternating spells of adrenal stimulation and insulin coma as the Great Interrupter, the Village Explainer, the champion of Mental Jotto, the Free Analyst, Mr. Let's Find Out, leads the troops on a seventy-two-hour forced march through the lateral geniculate and the pyramids of Betz, no breathers allowed, until every human brain is reduced finally to a clump of dried seaweed inside a burnt-out husk and collapses, implodes, in one last crunch of terminal boredom. Mr. Pull! Mr. Push! Mr. Auricularis! . . . But how could the Black Panther Party of America know that? Just now Lenny looks so sunk-down-low in the easy chair. Almost at Don Cox's feet he is, way down in an easy chair with his turtleneck and blazer on, and his neckpiece. Also right down front, on the couch next to the wall, is Otto Preminger, no piece of wallpaper himself, with his great head and neck rising up like a howitzer shell from out of his six-button double-breasted, after the manner of the eternal Occupation Zone commandant.

"Tell why," says Lenny.

"Well," says Cox, "that gets into the whole history of the church in the black community. It's a long story."

"Go ahead and tell it," says Lenny.

"Well," says Cox, "when the slaves were brought to America, they were always met at the boat by the cat with the whip and the gun . . . see . . . and along with him was the black preacher, who said, Everything's gonna be all right, as long as you're right with Jesus. It's like, the normal thing in the black community. The preacher was always the go-between the slavemasters and the slave, and the preacher would get a little extra crumb off the table for performing this service . . . you know . . . It's the same situation in the black community today. The preacher is riding around in a gold Cadillac, but it's the same thing. If you ask a lot of these churches to start working for the people instead of for The Man, they start worrying about that crumb . . . see . . . Because if the preacher starts working for the people, then the power structure starts harassing him. Like we found this one minister who was willing for us to use his church for the breakfast program. So okay, and then one day he comes in, and he's terrified . . . see . . . and he says we have to leave, that's all there is to it. The cat's terrified . . . So we say, okay, we'll leave, but just tell us what they said to you. Tell us what they did to intimidate you. But he won't even talk about it, he just says, Leave. He's too terrified to even talk about it."

Bernstein says, "Don, what's really worrying a lot of us here is the friction between groups like the Black Panthers and the established black community."

No problem. Cox says, "We recognize that there is not only a racial struggle going on in this country, but a class struggle. The class structure doesn't exist in the same way in the black community, but what we have are very bourgeois-minded people"—he uses the standard New Left pronunciation, which is "boooooooozh-wah"—"petty bourgeois-minded people . . . you see . . . and they have the same mentality as bourgeois-minded people in the white power structure."

"Yes," says Bernstein, "but a lot of us here are worried about things like threats against the lives of leaders of the established black community—"

Suddenly Rick Haynes speaks out from the back of the room: "This thing about 'the black community' galls me!" He's really put out, but it's hard to tell what over, because what he does is look down at the Ash-Blond Beauty, who is only about ten feet away: "This *lovely young lady* here was asking about *what she could do* . . ." What a look . . . if sarcasm could reach 550 degrees, she would shrivel up like a slice of Oscar Mayer bacon. "Well, I suggest that she forget about going into *the black community*. I suggest that she think about the white community. Like the *Wall Street Journal*—the *Wall Street Jour-*

nal just printed an article about the Black Panthers, and they came to the shocking conclusion—for them—that a majority of the black community supports the Black Panthers. Well, I suggest that this lovely young lady get somebody like her *daddy,* who just might have a little more *pull* than she does, to call up the *Wall Street Journal* and congratulate them when they write it straight like that. Just call up and say, We like that. The name of the game is to use the media, because the media have been using us."

"Right on," says Don Cox.

Curiously, Ash Blonde doesn't seem particularly taken aback by all this. If this dude in a pinstripe suit thinks he's going to keep her off The All-Weather Panther Committee, he's bananas . . .

And if they think this is going to deflect Leonard Bernstein, they're *all* out to lunch. About five people are talking at once—Quat—Lefcourt—Lenny—Cox—Barbara Walters is on the edge of her chair, bursting to ask a question—but it is the Pastmaster who cuts through:

"I want to know what the Panthers' attitude is toward the threats against these black leaders!" says Lenny.

Lefcourt the lawyer jumps up: "Mr. Bernsteen—"

"*STEIN!*" roars Lenny. He's become a veritable tiger, except that he is sunk down so low into the Margaret Owen billows of the easy chair, with his eyes peering up from way down in the downy hollow, that everything he says seems to be delivered into the left knee of Don Cox.

"Mr. Bernstein," says Lefcourt, "every time there are threats, every time there is violence, it's used as an indictment of the Black Panthers, even if they had nothing whatsoever to do with it."

"I'm hip," says Lenny. "That's what I'm trying to establish. I just want to get an answer to the question."

Lefcourt, Quat, half a dozen people it seems like, are talking, telling Lenny how the threats he is talking about, against Whitney Young and Roy Wilkins, were in 1967, before the Panthers were even in existence in New York, and the people arrested in the so-called conspiracy allegedly belonged to an organization called Revolutionary Action Movement, and how the cops, the newspapers, TV, like to aim everything at the Panthers.

"I think everybody in this room buys that," says Bernstein, "and everybody buys the distinction between what the media, what the newspapers and television say about the Panthers and what they really are. But this thing of the threats is in our collective memory. Bayard Rustin was supposed to be here tonight, but he isn't here, and for an important reason. The reason he isn't here tonight is that he was warned that his life would be in danger, and that's what I want to know about."

It's a gasper, this remark. Lefcourt and Quat start talking, but then, suddenly, before Don Cox can open his mouth, Lenny reaches up from out of the depths of the easy chair and hands him a mint. There it is, rising up on the tips of his fingers, a mint. It is what is known as a puffed mint, an after-dinner mint, of the sort that suddenly appears on the table in little silver Marthinsen bowls, as if deposited by the mint fairy, along with the coffee, but before the ladies leave the room, a mint so small, fragile, angel-white, and melt-crazed that you have to pick it up with the tips of your forefinger and thumb lest it get its thing on a straightaway, namely, one tiny sweet salivary peppermint melt... in mid-air, so to speak... just so... Cox takes the mint and stares at Bernstein with a strange Plexiglas gaze . . . This little man sitting down around his kneecaps with his Groovy gear and love beads on . . .

Finally Cox comes around. "We don't know anything about that," he says. "We don't threaten anybody. Like, we only advocate violence in self-defense, because we are a colonial people in a capitalist country . . . you know? . . . and the only thing we can do is defend ourselves against oppression."

Quat is trying to steer the whole thing away—but suddenly Otto Preminger speaks up from the sofa where he's sitting, also just a couple of feet from Cox: "He used one important word"—then he looks at Cox—"you said zis is de most repressive country in de world. I dun't be*leef* zat."

Cox says, "Let me answer the question—"

Lenny breaks in: "When you say 'capitalist' in that pejorative tone, it reminds me of Stokely. When you read Stokely's statement in *The New York Review of Books,* there's only one place where he says what he really means, and that's way down in paragraph 28 or something, and you realize he is talking about setting up a socialist government—"

Preminger is still talking to Cox: "Do you mean dat zis government is more repressive zan de government of Nigeria?"

"I don't know anything about the government of Nigeria," says Cox. "Let me answer the question—"

"You dun't eefen *lis*ten to de kvestion," says Preminger. "How can you *answer* de kvestion?"

"Let me answer the question," Cox says, and he says to Lenny: "We believe that the government is obligated to give every man employment or a guaranteed income . . . see . . . but if the white businessman will not give full employment, then the means of production should be taken from the businessman and placed in the community, with the people."

Lenny says: "How? I dig it! But how?"

"Right on!" Someone in the back digs it, too.

"Right on!"

Julie Belafonte pipes up: "That's a very difficult question!"

"You can't blueprint the future," says Cox.

"You mean you're just going to *wing* it?" says Lenny.

"Like . . . this is what we want, man," says Cox. "We want the same thing as you, we want peace. We want to come home at night and be with the family . . . and turn on the TV . . . and smoke a little *weed* . . . you know? . . . and get a little *high* . . . you dig? . . . and we'd like to get into that bag, like anybody else. But we can't do that . . . see . . . because if they send in the pigs to rip us off and brutalize our families, then we have to fight."

"I couldn't agree with you more!" says Lenny. "But what do you do—"

Cox says: "We think that this country is going more and more toward fascism to oppress those people who have the will to fight back—"

"I agree with you one hundred percent!" says Lenny. "But you're putting it in defensive terms, and don't you really mean it in offensive terms—"

"That's the language of the oppressor," says Cox. "As soon as—"

"Dat's not—" says Preminger.

"Let me finish!" says Cox. "As a Black Panther, you get used to—"

"Dat's not—"

"Let me finish! As a Black Panther, you learn that language is used as an instrument of control, and—"

"He doesn't *mean* dat!"

"Let me finish!"

Cox to Preminger to Bernstein to . . . they're wrestling for the Big Ear . . . quite a struggle . . . Cox standing up by the piano covered in the million-dollar *chatchkas* . . . Lenny sunk down into the Margaret Owen easy chair . . . Preminger, the irresistible commandant of the sofa . . . they're pulling and tugging—

—whereupon the little gray man, the servant of history, pops up from beside the other piano and says: "Mr. Bernstein, will you yield the floor to Mrs. Bernstein?"

And suddenly Felicia, serene and flawless as Mary Astor, is on her feet: "I would just like to quote this passage from Richard Harris, in *The New Yorker*," and she is standing up beside the other piano with a copy of *The New Yorker* in her hand, reading from an article by Richard Harris on the Justice Department.

"This is a letter from Roger Wilkins to Secretary Finch," says Felicia. This is Roy Wilkins's nephew, Roger Wilkins, former head of the Justice Department's Community Relations Service, and now with the Ford Foundation. " 'A year ago I figured that a black rebellion was out of the question, because black leaders—even the most militant of them—knew that all they would accomplish was to get themselves and their followers killed.' " Felicia looks up at the audience, as during any first-class reading, and her voice begins to take on more and more theatrical lift. " 'But I think that the despair is far deeper now. You just can't go on seeing how white men live, the opportunity they have, listening to all the promises they make and realizing how little they have delivered, without having to fight an almost ungovernable rage within yourself.' " Felicia's voice has taken on the very vibrato of emotion. And in the back of the room, standing close to Gail Lumet, is Roger Wilkins himself. " 'Some black children in this country,' " recites Felicia, " 'have to eat dog food or go hungry. No man can go on watching his children grow up in hunger and misery like that, with wealth and comfort on every side of him, and continue to regard himself as a man. I think that there are black men who have enough pride now so that they would rather die than go on living the way they have to live. And I think that most of us moderates would have difficulty arguing with them. The other day, an old friend of mine, a black man who has spent his life trying to work things out for his people within the system, said to me' "—Felicia looks at the audience and sets up the clincher—" ' *"Roger, I'm going to get a gun. I can't help it."* ' "

"That's marrrrrrrr-velous!" says Lenny. He says it with profound emotion . . . He sighs . . . He sinks back into the easy chair . . . Richard Harris . . . Ahura Mazda with the original flaming revelation . . .

Cox seizes the moment: "Our Minister of Defense, Huey P. Newton, has said if we can't find a meaningful life . . . you know . . . maybe we can have a meaningful death . . . and one reason the power structure fears the Black Panthers is that they know the Black Panthers are ready to die for what they believe in, and a lot of us have already died."

Lenny seems like a changed man. He looks up at Cox and says, "When you walk into this house, into this building"— and he gestures vaguely as if to take it all in, the moldings, the sconces, the Roquefort morsels rolled in crushed nuts, the servants, the elevator attendant and the doormen downstairs in their white dickeys, the marble lobby, the brass struts on the marquee out front—"when you walk into this house, you must feel infuriated!"

Cox looks embarrassed. "No, man . . . I manage to overcome that . . . That's a personal thing . . . I used to get very uptight about things like that, but—"

"Don't you get bitter? Doesn't that make you mad?"

"Noooo, man . . . That's a personal thing . . . see . . . and I don't get mad about that personally. I'm over that."

"Well," says Lenny, "it makes *me* mad!"

And Cox stares at him, and the Plexiglas lowers over his eyes once more . . . These cats—if I wasn't here to see it—

"This is a very paradoxical situation," says Lenny. "Having this apartment makes this meeting possible, and if this apartment didn't exist, you wouldn't have it. And yet—well, it's a very paradoxical situation."

"I don't get uptight about all that," says Cox. "I've been through all that. I grew up in the country, in a farming community, and I finally became a 'respectable Negro' . . . you know . . . I did all the right things. I got a job and a car, and I was wearing a suit and getting good pay, and as long as I didn't break any rules I could go to work and wear my suit and get paid. But then one day it dawned on me that I was only kidding myself, because that wasn't where it was at. In a society like ours I might as well have had my hairguard on and my purple pants, because when I walked down the street I was just another *nigger* . . . see . . . just another *nigger* . . . But I don't have that hate thing going. Like, I mean, I can *feel* it, I can *get* uptight. Like the other day I was coming out of the courthouse in Queens and there was this off-duty pig going by . . . see . . . and he gives me the finger. That's the pig's way of letting you know he's got his eye on you. He gives me the finger . . . and for some reason or other, this kind of got the old *anger* boiling . . . you know?"

"God," says Lenny, and he swings his head around toward the rest of the room, "most of the people in this room have had a problem about being unwanted!"

Most of the people in this room have had a problem about being unwanted. There it is. It's an odd feeling. Most-of-the-people-in-this-room's . . . heads have just spun out over this one. Lenny is unbeatable. Mental Jotto at 3 a.m. He has done it. He has just steered the Black Panther movement into a 1955 Jules Feiffer cartoon. Rejection, Security, Anxiety, Oedipus, Electra, Neurosis, Transference, Id, Superego, Archetype and Field of Perception, that wonderful 1950's game, beloved by all educated young men and women in the East who grew up in the era of the great cresting tide of Freud, Jung, Adler, Reik & Reich, when everyone either had an analyst or quoted Ernest Dichter telling Maytag that dishwashing machines were bought by women with anal compulsions. And in the gathering insulin coma Lenny has the Panthers and seventy-five assorted celebrities and culturati heading off on the long march into the neural jungle, 1955 Forever. One way or another we *all* feel insecure—right? And so long as we repress our—it's marvelous! Mr. Auricularis! The Village Explainer! *Most of the people in this room have had a problem about being unwanted—*

Cox looks at him, with the Plexiglas lowering . . . But the little gray man, the servant of history, jumps in once more. He sends a lovely young thing, one of the blondes in the room, over to whisper something in Lenny's ear. "Livingston Wingate is here," she tells him.

No slouch in such situations, Lenny immediately seems to dope this out as just an interruption to shut him up.

"Oh, why don't I just leave!" he says. He makes a mock move as if to get up from the chair and leave the room. "Noooo! Noooo!" everybody says. Everybody is talking at once, but then Barbara Walters, who has had this certain thing building up inside of her, springs it loose. Everybody knows that voice, Barbara Walters of the *Today Show,* televised coast to coast every morning, a mid-Atlantic voice, several miles east of Newfoundland and heading for Blackpool, and she leans forward, sitting in the third row in her checked pants suit with the great fur collar:

"I'm a member of the news media, but I'm here as an individual, because I'm concerned about the questions raised here, and there has been a lot of talk about the media. Last year we interviewed Mrs. Eldridge Cleaver, Kathleen Cleaver, and it was not an edited report or anything of that sort. She had a chance to say whatever she wanted, and this is a very knowledgeable, very brilliant, very articulate woman ... And I asked her, I said, 'I have a child, and you have a child,' and I said, 'Do you see any possibility that our children will be able to grow up and live side by side in peace and harmony?' and she said, 'Not with the conditions that prevail in this society today, not without the overthrow of the system.' So I asked her, 'How do you feel, as a mother, about the prospect of your child being in that kind of confrontation, a nation in flames?' and she said, 'Let it burn!' And I said, 'What about your own child?' and she said, 'May he light the first match!' And that's what I want to ask you about. I'm still here as a concerned person, not as a reporter, but what I'm talking about, and what Mr. Bernstein and Mr. Preminger are talking about, when they ask you about the way you refer to capitalism, is whether you see any chance at all for a peaceful solution to these problems, some way out without violence."

Cox says, "Not with the present system. I can't see that. Like, what can change? There's 750 families that own all the wealth of this country—"

"Dat's not *tdrue!*" says Preminger. "Dere are many people wid wealth all over—"

"Let me finish!—and these families are the most reactionary elements in the country. A man like H. L. Hunt wouldn't let me in his house."

Barbara Walters says: "I'm not talking about—"

"I wouldn't *go* to his house eef he *asked me,*" says Preminger.

"Well I almost—"

"What about Ross Perot? He's a Texan, too, and is spending millions of dollars trying to get de vives of prisoners of war in touch wid de government of North Vietnam—"

Cox says: "I would respect him more if he was giving his money to hungry children."

"He is!" says Preminger. "He is! You dun't *read* anyt'ing! Dat's your tdrouble!"

"I'm not talking about that," Barbara Walters says to Cox. "I'm talking about what's supposed to happen to other people if you achieve your goals."

"You can't just put it like that!" says Julie Belafonte. "That needs clarification."

Barbara Walters says: "I'm talking as a white woman who

has a white husband, who is a capitalist, or an agent of capitalists, and I am, too, and I want to know if you are to have your freedom, does that mean we have to go!"

Barbara Walters and her husband, Lee Guber, a producer, up against the wall in the cellar in Ekaterinburg—

Cox says, "For one person to be free, everybody must be free. As long as one whole class is oppressed, there is no freedom in a society. A lot of young white people are beginning to—"

"Dat eesn't what she's asking—"

"Let me finish—let me answer the question—"

"You dun't even *lis*ten to de kvestion—"

"Let me finish— A lot of young white people are beginning to understand about oppression. They're part of the petty bourgeoisie. It's a different class from the black community, but there's a common oppressor. They're protesting about individual freedoms, to have their music and smoke weed and have sex. These are individual freedoms but they are beginning to understand—"

"If you're for freedom," says Preminger, "tell me dis: Is it all right for a Jew to leave Russia and settle in Israel?"

"Let me finish—"

"Is it all right for a Jew to leave Russia and settle in Israel?"

Most people in the room don't know what the hell Preminger is driving at, but Leon Quat and the little gray man know right away. They're trying to wedge into the argument. The hell with that little number, that Israel and Al Fatah and U.A.R. and MIG's and U.S.S.R. and Zionist imperialist number—not in this room you don't—

Quat stands up with a terrific one-big-happy-family smile on and says: "I think we're all ready to agree that the crisis in this country today comes not from the Black Panthers but from the war in Vietnam, and—"

But there is a commotion right down front. Barbara Walters is saying something to one of the Panther wives, Mrs. Lee Berry, in the front row.

"What did she say to you?" says Lenny.

"I was talking to this very nice lady," says Barbara Walters, "and she said, 'You sound like you're afraid.' "

Mrs. Berry laughs softly and shakes her head.

"I'm not afraid of you," Barbara Walters says to her, "but maybe I am about the idea of the death of my children!"

"Please!" says Quat.

"All I'm asking is if we can work together to create justice without violence and destruction!"

"Please!" says Quat.

"He never answered her kvestion!" says Preminger.

"Please!"

"I can answer the question—"

"You dun't eefen *lis*ten—"

"So—"

"Let me answer the question! I can deal with that. We don't believe that it will happen within the present system, but—"

Lenny says: "So you're going to start a revolution from a Park Avenue apartment!"

Right on!

Quat sings out desperately: "Livingston Wingate is here! Can we please have a word from Mr. Livingston Wingate of the Urban League?" Christ, yes, bring in Livingston Wingate.

So Livingston Wingate, executive director of the New York Urban League, starts threading his way down to the front. He hasn't got the vaguest notion of what has been going on, except that this is Panther night at the Bernsteins'. He apparently thinks he is called upon to wax forensic, because he starts into a long disquisition on the changing mood of black youth.

"I was on television this morning with a leader of the Panther movement," he says, "and—"

"That was me"—Cox from his chair beside the piano.

Wingate wheels around. "Oh, yes..." He does a double take. "I didn't see you here... That was *you*... Hah..." And then he continues, excoriating himself and his generation of black leaders for their failures, because non-violence didn't work, and he can no longer tell the black youth not to throw that rock—

In the corner, meanwhile, by the piano, Preminger has reached out and grabbed Cox by the forearm in some kind of grip of goodwill and brotherhood and is beaming as if to say, I didn't mean anything by it, and Cox is trying to grab his hand and shake hands and say that's O.K., and Preminger keeps going for the forearm, and Cox keeps going for the hand, and they're lost there in a weird eccentric tangle of fingers and wrist bones between the sofa and grand piano, groping and tugging—

—because, says Livingston Wingate, he cannot prove to the ghetto youth that anything else will work, and so forth and so on, "and they are firmly convinced that there can be no change unless the system is changed."

"Less than five percent of the people of this country have ninety percent of the wealth," says Lefcourt the lawyer, "and ten percent of them have most of the ninety percent. The mass of the people by following the system can never make changes, and there is no use continuing to tell people about constitutional guarantees, either. Leon and I could draw up a constitution that would give us all the power, and we could make it so deep and legitimate that you would have to kill us to change it!"

Julie Belafonte rises up in front and says: "Then we'll kill you!"

"Power to the people!" says Leon Quat . . . and all rise to their feet . . . and Charlotte Curtis puts the finishing touches in her notebook . . . and the white servants wait patiently in the wings to wipe the drink rings off the Amboina tables . . .

STILL WOUND UP WITH THE EXCITEMENT OF THE MENTAL Jotto they had all just been through, Lenny, Felicia, and Don Cox kept on talking there in the duplex, long after most guests had gone, up to about 10 p.m., in fact. Lenny and Felicia knew they had been through a unique experience, but they had no idea of the furor that was going to break the next day when Charlotte Curtis's account of the party appeared in *The New York Times.*

The story appeared in two forms—a preliminary report rushed through for the first edition, which reaches the streets about 10:30 p.m., and a much fuller one for the late city edition, the one most New Yorkers see in the morning. Neither account was in any way critical of what had gone on. Even after reading them, Lenny and Felicia probably had little inkling of what was going to happen next. The early version began:

"Mrs. Leonard Bernstein, who has raised money for such diverse causes as indigent Chileans, the New York Philharmonic, Church World Service, Israeli student scholarships, emotionally disturbed children, the New York Civil Liberties Union, a Greek boys' school and Another Mother for Peace, was into what she herself admitted yesterday was a whole new thing. She gave a cocktail party for the Black Panthers. 'Not a frivolous party,' she explained before perhaps 30 guests arrived, 'but a chance for all of us to hear what's happening to them. They've really been treated very inhumanely.' "

Felicia herself couldn't have asked for it to be put any better. In the later edition it began: "Leonard Bernstein and a Black Panther leader argued the merits of the Black Panther party's philosophy before nearly 90 guests last night in the Bernsteins' elegant Park Avenue duplex"—and went on to give some of the dialogue of Lenny's, Cox's and Preminger's argument over Panther tactics and Lenny's refrain of "I dig it." There was also a picture of Cox standing beside the piano and talking to the group, with Felicia in the background. No one in the season of Radical Chic could have asked for better coverage. It took up a whole page in the fashion section, along with ads for B. Altman's, Edith Imre wigs, fur coats, the Sherry-Netherland Hotel, and The Sun and Surf (Palm Beach).

What the Bernsteins probably did not realize at first was that the story was going out on *The New York Times* News Service wires. In other cities throughout the United States and Europe it was played on page one, typically, to an international chorus of horse laughs or nausea, depending on one's *Weltanschauung*. The English, particularly, milked the story for all it was worth and seemed to derive one of the great cackles of the year from it.

By the second day, however—Friday—the Bernsteins certainly knew they were in for it. The *Times* ran an editorial on the party. It was headed "False Note on Black Panthers":

"Emergence of the Black Panthers as the romanticized darlings of the politico-cultural jet set is an affront to the majority of black Americans. This so-called party, with its confusion of Mao-Marxist ideology and Fascist para-militarism, is fully entitled to protection of its members' constitutional rights. It was to make sure that those rights are not abridged by persecution masquerading as law-enforcement that a committee of distinguished citizens has recently been formed [a group headed by Arthur Goldberg that sought to investigate the killing of Fred Hampton by Chicago police].

"In contrast, the group therapy plus fund-raising soiree at the home of Leonard Bernstein, as reported in this newspaper yesterday, represents the sort of elegant slumming that degrades patrons and patronized alike. It might be dismissed as guilt-relieving fun spiked with social consciousness, except for its impact on those blacks and whites seriously working for complete equality and social justice. It mocked the memory of Martin Luther King Jr., whose birthday was solemnly observed throughout the nation yesterday.

"Black Panthers on a Park Avenue pedestal create one more distortion of the Negro image. Responsible black leadership is not likely to cheer as the Beautiful People create a new myth that Black Panther is beautiful."

Elegant slumming ... mocked the memory of Martin Luther King ... Black Panthers on a Park Avenue pedestal ... the Beautiful People ... it was a stunner. And this was not the voice of some right-wing columnist like William Buckley (although he would be heard from)—this was an editorial, on the editorial page, underneath the eagle medallion with "All the News That's Fit to Print" and "Established 1851" on it ... in the very *New York Times* itself.

Felicia spoke to Charlotte Curtis, and Charlotte Curtis

agreed with her that the *Times* was wrong to characterize the party as "elegant slumming." The following week she wrote a story testifying to the sincerity of many society figures, including Felicia, who had worked diligently for the less fortunate. But she stood by her original story down to the last detail. Felicia seemed to accept this in good grace. But Lenny was not so sure. The whole thing sounded like a put-up job. Look at it this way: they held a meeting—not a party, but a meeting—in his home on one of the most important issues of the day, and the *Times* chose to run a story not by Homer Bigart or Harrison Salisbury but a Society writer who puts in a lot of "hairbrained" details about his Black Watch pants and a lot of sappy quotes he never uttered—right? This sets him up like a dummy for a roundhouse right from the cheap seats—the editorial about "elegant slumming" and the mockery of the memory of Martin Luther King. Not only that, he himself was already beginning to be mocked in New York in the old word-of-mouth carnival. It was unbelievable. Cultivated people, intellectuals, were characterizing him as "a masochist" and—and this was the really cruel part—as "the David Susskind of American Music."

Felicia sat down that very day, Friday, and wrote an aggrieved but calmly worded letter to the *Times:*

"As a civil libertarian, I asked a number of people to my house on Jan. 14 in order to hear the lawyer and others involved with the Panther 21 discuss the problem of civil liberties as applicable to the men now waiting trial, and to help raise funds for their legal expenses.

"Those attending included responsible members of the black leadership as well as distinguished citizens from a variety of walks of life, all of whom share common concern on the subject of civil liberties and equal justice under our laws.

"The outcome of the Panther 21 trial will be determined by the judge and jury. That was not our concern. But the ability of the defendants to prepare a proper defense will depend on the help given prior to the trial, and this help must not be denied because of lack of funds.

"It was for this deeply serious purpose that our meeting was called. The frivolous way in which it was reported as a 'fashionable' event is unworthy of the *Times,* and offensive to all people who are committed to humanitarian principles of justice."

Felicia delivered the letter in person to the *Times* that afternoon. The Bernsteins picked up Saturday's paper—and no letter. In fact, it did not appear until Wednesday, *after* the publication of a letter from someone named Porter saying things like "we shall soon witness the birth of local Rent-a-Panther organizations." This fed the conspiracy theory, at least in the Bernstein household. By now columnists all over the place were taking their whack at the affair. Buckley, for example, cited it as an object lesson in the weird masochism of the white liberal who bids the Panther come devour him in his "luxurious lair."

But if the Bernsteins thought their main problem at this point was a bad press, they were wrong. A controversy they were apparently oblivious of suddenly erupted around them. Namely, the bitterness between Jews and blacks over an issue that had been building for three years, ever since Black Power became important. The first inkling the Bernsteins had was when they started getting hate mail, some of it apparently from Jews of the Queens-Brooklyn Jewish Defense League variety. Then the League's national chairman, Rabbi Meir Kahane, blasted Lenny publicly for joining a "trend in liberal and intellectual circles to lionize the Black Panthers . . . We defend the right of blacks to form defense groups, but they've gone beyond this to a group which hates other people. That's not nationalism, that's Naziism. And if Bernstein and other such intellectuals do not know this, they know nothing."

The Jewish Defense League had been formed in 1968 for the specific purpose of defending Jews in Low Rent neighborhoods, many of which are black. But even many wealthier and more cultivated Jews, who look at the Defense League as somewhat extremist, plebeian, and gauche, agreed essentially with the point Kahane was making. One of the ironies of the history of the Jews in America was that their long championship of black civil liberties had begun to backfire so badly in the late 1960's. As Seymour Lipset has put it, "The integrationist movement was largely an alliance between Negroes and Jews (who, to a considerable extent, actually dominated it). Many of the interracial civil-rights organizations have been led and financed by whites, and the majority of their white members have been Jews. Insofar as a Negro effort emerged to break loose from involvement with whites, from domination of the civil-rights struggle by white liberals, it meant concretely a break with Jews, for they were the whites who were active in these movements. The Black Nationalist leadership had to push whites (Jews) 'out of the way,' and to stop white (Jewish) 'interference' in order to get whites (Jews) 'off their backs.' "

Meanwhile, Black Power groups such as SNCC and the Black Panthers were voicing support for the Arabs against Israel. This sometimes looked like a mere matter of black nationalism; after all, Egypt was a part of Africa, and black-nationalist literature sometimes seemed to identify the Arabs as blacks fighting the white Israelis. Or else it looked like merely a commitment to world socialism; the Soviet Union and China supported the Arabs against the imperialist tools, the Israelis. But many Jewish leaders regarded the anti-Zionist stances of groups like the Panthers as a veiled American-brand anti-Semitism, tied up with such less theoretical matters as extortion, robbery, and mayhem by blacks against Jews in ghetto areas. They cited things like the August 30, 1969, issue of *Black Panther,* which carried an article entitled "Zionism (Kosher Nationalism) + Imperialism = Fascism" and spoke of "the fascist Zionist pigs." The article was signed "Field Marshal D.C.," which may have stood for Field Marshal Don Cox. The June 1967 issue of *Black Power,* a publication of a different organization, the Black Panther Party of Northern California, had carried a poem entitled "Jew-Land," which said:

> *Jew-Land, On a summer afternoon*
> *Really, Couldn't kill the Jews too soon,*
> *Now dig. The Jews have stolen our bread*
> *Their filthy women tricked our men into bed*
> *So I won't rest until the Jews are dead . . .*
> *In Jew-Land, Don't be a Tom on Israel's side*
> *Really, Cause that's where Christ was crucified.*

But in the most literate circles of the New Left—well, the Panthers' pronouncements on foreign affairs couldn't be taken too seriously. Ideologically, they were still feeling their way around. To be a UJA Zionist about the whole thing was to be old-fashioned, middle-class, middle-aged, suburban, Ocean-sided, Cedarhurstian, in an age when the youth of the New Left had re-programmed the whole circuitry of left opposition to oppression. The main thing was that the Panthers were the legitimate vanguard of the black struggle for liberation—among the culturati whom Leonard Bernstein could be expected to know and respect, this was not a point of debate, it was an axiom. The chief theoretical organ of Radical Chic, *The New York Review of Books,* regularly cast Huey Newton and Eldridge Cleaver as the Simón Bolívar and José Martí of the black ghettos. On August 24, 1967, *The New York Review of Books* paid homage to the summer urban riot season by printing a diagram for the making of a Molotov cocktail on its front page. In fact, the journal was sometimes referred to good-naturedly as *The Parlour Panther,* with the *-our* spelling of *Parlour* being an allusion to its concurrent motif of Anglophilia. The *Review*'s embracing of such apparently contradictory attitudes—the nitty-gritty of the ghetto warriors and the preciosity of traditional English Leavis & Empson intellectualism—was really no contradiction at all, of course. It was merely the essential double-track mentality of Radical Chic—*nostalgie de la boue* and high protocol—in its literary form. In any case, given all this, people like Lenny and Felicia could hardly have been expected to comprehend a complex matter like the latter-day friction between blacks and Jews.

To other people involved in Radical Chic, however, the picture was now becoming clear as day. This was no time for Custer's last stand. This was time . . . to panic. Two more couples had already agreed to give parties for the Panthers: Peter and Cheray Duchin and Frank and Domna Stanton. The

Duchins had already gotten some of the static themselves. Peter had gone to Columbus, Ohio, with his orchestra . . . and the way some of the locals let him have it! All because Charlotte Curtis's article had quoted Cheray saying how thrilled she was at the prospect of meeting her first Black Panther at Felicia's. Columbus freaking *Ohio,* yet. Nor did it take the Stantons long to put two and two together. Frank Stanton, the entrepreneur, not the broadcaster, had a duplex co-op that made Lenny's look like a fourth-floor walkup. It had marble floors, apricot velvet walls, trompe-l'oeil murals in the dining room, the works. A few photos of the Panthers against this little backdrop—well, you could write the story yourself.

On Saturday evening, the twenty-fourth, the Duchins, the Stantons, Sidney and Gail Lumet, and Lenny and Felicia met at the Bernsteins' to try to think out the whole situation. Sidney Lumet was convinced that a new era of "McCarthyism" had begun. It was a little hard to picture the editorial and women's page staffs of the *Times* as the new Joe McCarthy—but damn it . . . The *Times* was pushing its own pet organizations, the NAACP, the Urban League, the Urban Coalition, and so on. Why did it look like the *Times* always tried to punish prominent Jews who refused to lie down and play good solid burghers? Who was it who said the *Times* was a Catholic newspaper run by Jews to fool the Protestants? Some professor at Columbia . . . In any case, they were now all "too exposed" to do the Panthers any good by giving parties for the Panthers in their homes. They would do better to work through organizations like the NAACP legal defense fund.

LENNY COULDN'T GET OVER THE WHOLE AFFAIR. EARLIER IN the evening he had talked to a reporter and told him it was "nauseating." The so-called "party" for the Panthers had not been a party at all. It had been a meeting. There was nothing social about it. As to whether he thought cause parties were held in the homes of socially prominent people simply because the living rooms were large and the acoustics were good, he didn't say. In any case, he and Felicia didn't give parties, and they didn't go to parties, and they were certainly not in anybody's "jet set." And they were not "masochists," either.

So four nights later Lenny, in a tuxedo, and Felicia, in a black dress, walked into a party in the triplex of one of New York's great hostesses, overlooking the East River, on the street of social dreams, East 52nd, and right off the bat some woman walks right up to him and says, "Lenny, I just think you're a masochist." It was unbelievable.

But by the twenty-fourth, ten days after the Panther night, Lenny's distress was easily matched by Elinor Guggenheimer's. She had already sent out invitations to a party for the Young Lords in her duplex the following day, Sunday the twenty-fifth. This was a fine situation. The Young Lords were in some ways Spanish Harlem's Puerto Rican equivalents of the Black Panthers and were, in fact, actually allied with the Panthers—and her duplex was just ten blocks up Park Avenue from the Bernsteins'. Elinor Guggenheimer's husband was Randolph Guggenheimer of the law firm of Guggenheimer & Untermyer. She had been a city planning commissioner and the head of many major charitable and educational organizations. Not only that, she was the running mate of Herman Badillo in his campaign for the Democratic nomination for mayor last year. Nobody was likely to write her off as a dilettante. Nevertheless, while the Bernsteins' duplex might be described in the *Times* as "elegant," hers would rank as sumptuous. There was enough aged and seasoned marble, fruitwood, and Oriental weaving in the place to illustrate one of those $30 Christmas books on décor through the ages.

Already newspaper and magazine writers, including Charlotte Curtis, had approached her about covering the event. She told them she wanted no press whatsoever. This was not for her sake, however. It was for the Young Lords'. Two things she repeated over and over. "Don't erect a barrier at 96th Street"—this being a Park Avenue allusion to the fact that the "good" part of the Upper East Side ends at 96th Street. "If you write about this, the Young Lords will never trust anyone south of 96th Street again." The other was: "It's not going to be a party. It's a meeting."

"In fact," she told one reporter, "if you're going to write about the meeting, then I'm not going to have it. I'm going to call it off. It wouldn't be fair to the Young Lords." Then she added: "I'm no jet-setter, and I don't go around to parties."

A whole new era, it was, for the duplex life of Park Avenue. Nobody gave parties. Nobody went to parties. Nobody was in anybody's alleged jet set. Ellie Guggenheimer was in good company there, and not just with Lenny. The fact is that only one person in the history of New York has ever publicly averred membership in "the jet set," and that was a young lady who was caught off-guard at the weird and disarming hour of 10 a.m. in the Zebra Room of El Morocco on February 3, 1965.

In any case, the party—meeting—was held the following afternoon, closed to the press. About a hundred people were admitted, including Felipe Luciano, leader of the Young Lords. According to one of Mrs. Guggenheimer's friends, a number of people who seemed "too social" were dis-invited as a precaution. The only raving socialites present were Carter and Amanda Burden, and they were legit, because he was a city councilman representing part of Spanish Harlem. Still, the party was a first for Radical Chic on Park Avenue. Mrs. Guggenheimer's helpers served up tossed salad and spaghetti. *Tossed salad and spaghetti* . . . the soul food of Radical Chic Panic.

The panic turned out to be good for The Friends of the Earth, somewhat the way the recession has been bad for the Four Seasons but good for Riker's. Many matrons, such as Cheray Duchin, turned their attention toward the sables, cheetahs, and leopards, once the Panthers became radioactive. The Stantons, meanwhile, dropped their plans for a Panther party and had one instead for the anti-Thieu & Ky Buddhists of Vietnam, and Richard Feigen dropped his plans for a party because of the Panthers' support for Al Fatah. Leonard Bernstein went off to England to rehearse with the London Symphony Orchestra for an already scheduled performance in the Royal Albert Hall. He couldn't have been very sorry about the trip. Unbelievable hostility was still bubbling around him. In Miami, Jewish pickets forced a moviehouse to withdraw a film of Lenny conducting the Israel Philharmonic on Mount Scopus in celebration of Israel's victory in the Six-Day War.

In general, the Radically Chic made a strategic withdrawal, denouncing the "witchhunt" of the press as they went. There was brief talk of a whole series of parties for the Panthers in and around New York, by way of showing the world that socialites and culturati were ready to stand up and be counted in defense of what the Panthers, and, for that matter, the Bernsteins, stood for. But it never happened. In fact, if the socialites already in line for Panther parties had gone ahead and given them in clear defiance of the opening round of attacks on the

Panthers and the Bernsteins, they might well have struck an extraordinary counterblow in behalf of the Movement. This is, after all, a period of great confusion among culturati and liberal intellectuals generally, and one in which a decisive display of conviction and self-confidence can be overwhelming. But for the Radically Chic to have fought back in this way would have been a violation of their own innermost convictions. Radical Chic, after all, is only radical in style; in its heart it is part of Society and its traditions. Politics, like Rock, Pop, and Camp, has its uses; but to put one's whole status on the line for *nostalgie de la boue* in any of its forms would be unprincipled.

Meanwhile, the damnable press dogged Lenny even in London. A United Press International reporter interviewed him there and sent out a story in which Lenny said: "They"— the Panthers—"are a bad lot. They have behaved very badly. They have laid their own graves. It was the Panthers themselves who spoiled the deal, they won't be rational." The next day Lenny told a *New York Times* reporter that the UPI story was "nonsense." He didn't remember what he had said, but he hadn't said anything like that. At the same time he released a statement that he had actually drawn up in New York before he left. It said that there had been no "party" for the Panthers in his home in the first place; it had been a "meeting," and the only concern at the meeting was civil liberties. "If we deny these Black Panthers their democratic rights because their philosophy is unacceptable to us, then we are denying our own democracy." He now made it clear that he was opposed to their philosophy, however. "It is not easy to discern a consistent political philosophy among the Black Panthers, but it is reasonably clear that they are advocating violence against their fellow citizens, the downfall of Israel, the support of Al Fatah and other similarly dangerous and ill-conceived pursuits. To all of these concepts I am vigorously opposed and will fight against them as hard as I can."

And still this damned nauseating furor would not lie down and die. Wouldn't you know it—two days after the, well, meeting, on the very day he and Felicia were reeling from the *Times* editorial, Daniel Patrick Moynihan, that renegade, had been down in Washington writing his famous "benign neglect" memo to Nixon. In it Moynihan had presented him and Felicia and their "party" as Exhibit A of the way black revolutionaries like the Panthers had become "culture heroes" of the Beautiful People. Couldn't you just see Nixon sitting in the Oval Room and clucking and fuming and muttering things like "rich snob bums" as he read: "You perhaps did not note on the society page of yesterday's *Times* that Mrs. Leonard Bernstein gave a cocktail party Wednesday to raise money for the Panthers. Mrs. W. Vincent Astor was among the guests. Mrs. Peter Duchin, 'the rich blond wife of the orchestra leader,' was thrilled. 'I've never met a Panther,' she said. 'This is a first for me.' "

On February 29 someone leaked the damned memo to the damned *New York Times,* and that did it. Now he was invested, installed, inaugurated, instituted, transmogrified as Mr. Parlour Panther for all time. The part about their "cocktail party" was right in the same paragraph with the phrase "benign neglect." And it didn't particularly help the situation that Mrs. Astor got off a rapid letter to the *Times* informing them that she was *not* at the "party." She received an invitation, like all sorts of other people, she supposed, but, in fact, she had *not* gone. Thanks a lot, Brooke Astor.

FOOLS, BOORS, PHILISTINES, BIRCHERS, B'NAI B'RITHEES, Defense Leaguers, Hadassah theater party piranhas, UJAviators, concert-hall Irishmen, WASP ignorati, toads, newspaper readers—they were booing him, Leonard Bernstein, the *egregio maestro . . . Boooooo.* No two ways about it. They weren't clearing their throats. They were squeezed into their $14.50 bequested seats, bringing up from out of the false bottoms of their bellies the old Low Rent raspberry boos of days gone by. *Boooooo.* Newspaper readers! That harebrained story in the *Times* had told how he and Felicia had given a party for the Black Panthers and how he had pledged a conducting fee to their defense fund, and now, stretching out before him in New York, was a great starched white-throated audience of secret candy-store bigots, greengrocer Moshe Dayans with patches over both eyes . . .

. . . once, after a concert in Italy, an old Italian, one of those glorious old Italians in an iron worsted black suit and a high collar with veritable embroideries of white thread mending the cracks where the collar folds over, one of those old Europeans who seem to have been steeped, aged, marinated, in centuries of true Culture in a land where people understood the art of *living* and the art of *feeling* and were not ashamed to express what was in their hearts—this old man had come up to him with his eyes brimming and his honest gnarled hands making imaginary snowballs and had said: "Egregio maestro! *Egreggggggggggggio maestro!*" The way he said it, combining the *egregio,* meaning "distinguished," with the *maestro,* meaning "master" . . . well, the way he said it meant a conductor so great, so brilliant, so dazzling, so transported, so transcendental, so—yes!—immortal ... well, there is no word in the whole lame dumb English language to describe it. And in that moment Leonard Bernstein knew that he had reached ...

—BOOOOOOOO! BOOOOOOOOO!

It was unbelievable. But it was real. These greengrocers— he was their whipping boy, and a bunch of $14.50 white-throated cretins were booing him, and it was no insomniac hallucination in the loneliness of 3 a.m.

Would that black apparition, that damnable Negro by the piano, be rising up from the belly of a concert grand for the rest of his natural life?

Mau-Mauing the Flak Catchers

GOING DOWNTOWN TO MAU-MAU THE BUREAUCRATS GOT to be the routine practice in San Francisco. The poverty program *encouraged* you to go in for mau-mauing. They wouldn't have known what to do without it. The bureaucrats at City Hall and in the Office of Economic Opportunity talked "ghetto" all the time, but they didn't know any more about what was going on in the Western Addition, Hunters Point, Potrero Hill, the Mission, Chinatown, or south of Market Street than they did about Zanzibar. They didn't know where to look. They didn't even know who to ask. So what could they do? Well . . . they used the Ethnic Catering Service . . . right . . . They sat back and waited for you to come rolling in with your certified angry militants, your guaranteed frustrated ghetto youth, looking like a bunch of wild men. Then you had your test confrontation. If you were outrageous enough, if you could shake up the bureaucrats so bad that their eyes froze into iceballs and their mouths twisted up into smiles of sheer physical panic, into shit-eating grins, so to speak— then they knew you were the real goods. They knew you were the right studs to give the poverty grants and community organizing jobs to. Otherwise they wouldn't know.

There was one genius in the art of confrontation who had mau-mauing down to what you could term a laboratory science. He had it figured out so he didn't even have to bring his boys downtown in person. He would just show up with a crocus sack full of revolvers, ice picks, fish knives, switchblades, hatchets, blackjacks, gravity knives, straight razors, hand grenades, blow guns, bazookas, Molotov cocktails, tank rippers, unbelievable stuff, and he'd dump it all out on somebody's shiny walnut conference table. He'd say, "These are some of the things I took off my boys last night . . . I don't know, man . . . Thirty minutes ago I talked a Panther out of busting up a cop . . ." And they would lay money on this man's ghetto youth patrol like it was now or never . . . The Ethnic Catering Service . . . Once they hired the Ethnic Catering Service, the bureaucrats felt like it was all *real*. They'd say to themselves, "We've given jobs to a hundred of the toughest hard-core youth in Hunters Point. The problem is on the way to being solved." They never inquired if the bloods they were giving the jobs to were the same ones who were causing the trouble. They'd say to themselves, "We don't have to find *them*. They find *us*" . . . Once the Ethnic Catering Service was on the case, they felt like they were reaching all those hard-to-reach hard-to-hold hardcore hardrock blackrage badass furious funky ghetto youth.

There were people in the Western Addition who practically

gave classes in mau-mauing. There was one man called Chaser. Chaser would get his boys together and he would give them a briefing like the U.S. Air Force wing commander gives his pilots in Thailand before they make the raid over North Vietnam, the kind of briefing where everybody is supposed to picture the whole mission like a film in their heads, the landmarks, the Red River, the approach pattern, the bombing run, every twist and turn, the SAM missile sites, the getaway, everything. In the same way Chaser would picture the room you would be heading into. It might be a meeting of the Economic Opportunity Council, which was the San Francisco poverty-program agency, or the National Alliance of Businessmen, which was offering jobs for the hard core, or the Western Regional Office of the Office of Economic Opportunity, or whatever, and he'd say:

"Now don't forget. When you go downtown, y'all wear your *ghetto rags* . . . see . . . Don't go down there with your Italian silk jerseys on and your brown suède and green alligator shoes and your Harry Belafonte shirts looking like some supercool toothpick-noddin' fool . . . you know . . . Don't nobody give a damn how pretty you can look . . . You wear your *combat* fatigues and your leather *pieces* and your shades . . . your *ghetto rags* . . . see . . . And don't go down there with your hair all done up nice in your curly Afro like you're messing around. You go down with your hair *stickin' out* . . . and *sittin' up*! Lookin' wild! I want to see you down there looking like a bunch of *wild niggers*!"

This Chaser was a talker. He used to be in vaudeville. At least that was what everybody said. That was how he learned to be such a beautiful talker. When the poverty program started, he organized his own group in the Western Addition, the Youth Coalition. Chaser was about forty, and he wasn't big. He was small, physically. But he knew how to make all those young aces of his take care of business. Chaser was black with a kind of brown hue. He had high cheekbones, like an Indian. He always wore a dashiki, over some ordinary pants and a Ban-Lon shirt. He had two of these Ban-Lon shirts and he alternated them. Anyway, he always wore the dashiki and a beret. He must not have had much hair on top of his head, because on the sides his hair stuck out like a natural, but the beret always laid flat. If he had as much hair on the top of his head as he had sticking out on the sides, that beret would have been sitting up in the air like the star on a Christmas tree. When everybody started wearing the Afros, it was hard on a lot of older men who were losing their hair. They would grow it long on the sides anyway and they would end up looking like that super-Tom on the Uncle Ben's rice box, or Bozo the Clown. Sometimes Chaser would wear a big heavy overcoat, one of those big long heavy double-breasted triple-button quadruple-lapel numbers like you see the old men wearing in Foster's Cafeteria. When you saw Chaser with that big coat on, over top of the dashiki, you'd have to smile, because then you knew Chaser wasn't in anybody's bag. Chaser was in Chaser's bag. That was all right, because you don't meet many men like Chaser. If there is any such thing as a born leader, he was one of them.

"Now, you women," he'd say. "I don't want you women to be macking with the brothers if they ain't tending to business. You women make your men get out of the house and get to work for the Youth Coalition. Don't you be macking around with nobody who ain't out working for the Youth Coalition. If he ain't man enough to be out on the street working for the people, then he ain't man enough for you to be macking around with."

This worked like a charm with the women and with the men, too. Chaser kept saying, "You women," but he was really talking to the men. He was challenging their masculinity. A lot of these young aces knew that their women thought they weren't man enough to stand up and make something out of themselves. And the women liked what he was saying, too, because he was including them in on the whole thing.

Then Chaser would say, "Now when we get there, I want you to come down front and stare at the man and don't say nothing. You just glare. No matter what he says. He'll try to get you to agree with him. He'll say, 'Ain't that right?' and 'You know what I mean?' and he wants you to say yes or nod your head . . . see . . . It's part of his psychological jiveass. But you don't say nothing. You just glare . . . see . . . Then some of the other brothers will get up on that stage behind him, like there's no more room or like they just gathering around. Then you brothers up there behind him, you start letting him have it . . . He starts thinking, 'Oh, good God! Those bad cats are in front of me, they all *around* me, they *behind* me. I'm sur-*round*ed.' That shakes 'em up.

"And then when one of the brothers is up talking, another brother comes up and whispers something in his ear, like this," and Chaser cups his hand around his mouth like he's whispering something. "And the brother stops talking, like he's listening, and the man thinks, 'What's he saying? What kind of unbelievable shit are they planning now?' The brother, he's not saying anything. He's just moving his lips. It's a tactic . . . you know . . . And at the end I'll slap my hand down on the desk—*whop*—and everybody gets up, like one man, and walks out of there. And that really shakes 'em up. They see that the people are unified, and disciplined, and mad, and tired of talking and ready for walking, and that shakes 'em up."

Chaser had his two main men, James Jones and Louis Downs. Downs was Chaser's showpiece. He was sharp. He was young and had a very athletic build. He had a haircut of the intellectual-natural variety and a pair of José Feliciano sunglasses and a black leather dashiki, and he'd have on a pair of A-1 racer pants. The A-1 racers are not just narrow, they're like a stovepipe, with the 16½-inch cuffs. And he'd have on either a pair of Vietnam combat boots with the green webbing or a pair of tennis shoes, but a really expensive kind of tennis shoe. You look at them and you know he really had to look especially hard to find that pair. He'd always be bracing his hands in front of him, pressing the heels of his hands together, which made the muscles pop up around his neck and his shoulders. James Jones was Chaser's philosopher. He was a talker, too. He'd come on like a Southern Christian Leadership preacher, giving all the reasons why, and then Downs would come on hard and really sharp. Between the three of them, Chaser and Downs and James Jones, they were like the Three Musketeers. They were beautiful to behold.

Chaser was funny. Just like he had everything planned out on his side, right down to the last detail, he thought the Man must have it planned out that far, too. Chaser had a kind of security paranoia. At a demonstration or something you'd see Chaser giving instructions to his boys with his hand over his mouth. He'd always be talking with his hand over his mouth, mumbling into his fingers, and he'd tell his boys to talk that way, too. Chaser was convinced that the Man had electronic eavesdropping devices trained on them. He'd tell you about the "parabolic earphones" and the deaf-mutes. He believed that the Man had trained a corps of deaf-mutes to read lips for crowd control. He'd have you believing it, too. It was like, What would *you* do if you were a deaf-mute and shuffling and shitkicking through life and the government comes along and offers to pay you money for reading lips and playing C.I.A. . . . Chaser didn't blame them any more than he'd blame a dog . . . They were being exploited like all the other Toms that didn't know any better . . .

BROTHERS LIKE CHASER WERE THE ONES WHO PERFECTED mau-mauing, but before long everybody in the so-called Third World was into it. Everybody was out mau-mauing up a storm, to see if they could win the victories the blacks had won. San Francisco, being the main port of entry for immigrants from all over the Pacific, had as many colored minorities as New York City. Maybe more. Blacks, Chicanos, Latinos, Chinese, Japanese, Filipinos, American Indians, Samoans—everybody was circling around the poverty program. By the end of 1968 there were eighty-seven different groups getting into the militant thing, getting into mau-mauing.

Nobody kept records on the confrontations, which is too bad. There must have been hundreds of them in San Francisco alone. Across the country there must have been thousands. When the confrontations touched the white middle class in a big way, like when black students started strikes and disruptions at San Francisco State, Columbia, Cornell, or Yale, or when somebody like James Forman came walking up to the pulpit of the Riverside Church carrying a four-pound cane the

size of the shillelagh the Fool Killer used to lug around to the
State Fair to kill fools with—when Forman got up there with
that hickory stick like he was going to swat all undeserving af-
fluent white Christians over the bean unless they paid five
hundred million dollars in reparations—then the media described it blow by blow. But what went on in the colleges and
churches was just a part of it. Bad dudes were out mau-
mauing at all the poverty agencies, at boards of education, at
city halls, hospitals, conventions, foundations, schools, chari-
ties, civic organizations, all sorts of places. It got to be an
American custom, like talk shows, *Face the Nation,* marriage
counseling, marathon encounters, or zoning hearings.

That was certainly the way the message came down to the
youth of the Third World in areas like the Mission, Chinatown, and Japan Town. Mau-mauing was the ticket. The confrontation route was the only road. So the Chinese, the
Japanese, the Chicanos, the Indians picked up on mau-mauing
from the bloods. Not only that, they would try to do it exactly
like the bloods. They'd talk like the bloods, dress like the
bloods, try to wear naturals like the bloods, even if their hair
was too straight to do it. There were Spanish and Oriental
dudes who washed their hair every day with Borax to make it
fluff up and sit out.

When anybody other than black people went in for mau-
mauing, however, they ran into problems, because the white
man had a different set of fear reflexes for each race he was
dealing with.

Whites didn't have too much fear of the Mexican-
American, the Chicano. The notion was that he was small,
placid, slow, no particular physical threat—until he grew his

hair Afro-style, talked like a blood or otherwise managed to seem "black" enough to raise hell. Then it was a different story.

The whites' physical fear of the Chinese was nearly zero. The white man pictured the Chinese as small, quiet, restrained little fellows. He had a certain deep-down voodoo fear of their powers of Evil in the Dark ... the Hatchet Men ... the Fangs of the Tong ... but it wasn't a live fear. For that matter, the young Chinese themselves weren't ready for the age of mau-mauing. It wasn't that they feared the white man, the way black people had. It was more that they didn't fear or resent white people enough. They looked down on whites as childish and uncultivated. They also found it somewhat shameful to present themselves as poor and oppressed, on the same level with Negroes and Mexican-Americans. It wasn't until 1969 that militants really got into confrontations in Chinatown.

Every now and then, after the poverty scene got going, and the confrontations became a regular thing, whites would run into an ethnic group they drew a total blank on, like the Indians or the Samoans. Well, with the Samoans they didn't draw a blank for long, not once they actually came up against them. The Samoans on the poverty scene favored the direct approach. They did not fool around. They were like the original unknown terrors. In fact, they were unknown terrors and a half.

Why so few people in San Francisco know about the Samoans is a mystery. All you have to do is see a couple of those Polynesian studs walking through the Mission, minding their own business, and you won't forget it soon. Have you ever by any chance seen professional football players in person, like on the street? The thing you notice is not just that they're big but that they are *so* big, it's weird. Everything about them is gigantic, even their heads. They'll have a skull the size of a watermelon, with a couple of little squinty eyes and a little mouth and a couple of nose holes stuck in, and no neck at all. From the ears down, the big yoyos are just one solid welded hulk, the size of an oil burner. You get the feeling that football players come from a whole other species of human, they're so big. Well, that will give you some idea of the Samoans, because they're bigger. The average Samoan makes Bubba Smith of the Colts look like a shrimp. They start out at about 300 pounds and from there they just get *wider.* They are big huge giants. Everything about them is wide and smooth. They have big wide faces and smooth features. They're a dark brown, with a smooth cast.

Anyway, the word got around among the groups in the Mission that the poverty program was going to cut down on summer jobs, and the Mission was going to be on the short end. So a bunch of the groups in the Mission got together and decided to go downtown to the poverty office and do some mau-mauing in behalf of the Mission before the bureaucrats made up their minds. There were blacks, Chicanos, Filipinos, and about ten Samoans.

The poverty office was on the first floor and had a big anteroom; only it's almost bare, nothing in it but a lot of wooden chairs. It looks like a union hall minus the spittoons, or one of those lobbies where they swear in new citizens. It's like they want to impress the poor that they don't have leather-top desks . . . All our money goes to you . . .

So the young aces from the Mission come trooping in, and they want to see the head man. The word comes out that the

No. 1 man is out of town, but the No. 2 man is coming out to talk to the people.

This man comes out, and he has that sloppy Irish look like Ed McMahon on TV, only with a longer nose. In case you'd like the local viewpoint, whites really have the noses . . . enormous, you might say . . . a whole bag full . . . long and pointed like carrots, goobered up like green peppers, hooked like a squash, hanging off the face like cucumbers . . . This man has a nose that is just on the verge of hooking over, but it doesn't quite make it.

"Have a seat, gentlemen," he says, and he motions toward the wooden chairs.

But he doesn't have to open his mouth. All you have to do is look at him and you get the picture. The man's a lifer. He's stone civil service. He has it all down from the wheatcolor Hush Puppies to the wash'n'dry semi-tab-collar shortsleeved white shirt. Those wheatcolor Hush Puppies must be like some kind of fraternal garb among the civil-service employees, because they all wear them. They cost about $4.99, and the second time you move your toes, the seams split and the tops come away from the soles. But they all wear them. The man's shirt looks like he bought it at the August end-of-summer sale at the White Front. It is one of those shirts with pockets on both sides. Sticking out of the pockets and running across his chest he has a lineup of ball-point pens, felt nibs, lead pencils, wax markers, such as you wouldn't believe, Paper Mates, Pentels, Scriptos, Eberhard Faber Mongol 482's, Dri-Marks, Bic PM-29's, everything. They are lined up across his chest like campaign ribbons.

He pulls up one of the wooden chairs and sits down on it. Only he sits down on it backwards, straddling the seat and hooking his arms and his chin over the back of the chair, like the head foreman in the bunkhouse. It's like saying, "We don't stand on ceremony around here. This is a shirtsleeve operation."

"I'm sorry that Mr. Johnson isn't here today," he says, "but he's not in the city. He's back in Washington meeting some important project deadlines. He's very concerned, and he would want to meet with you people if he were here, but right now I know you'll understand that the most important thing he can do for you is to push these projects through in Washington."

The man keeps his arms and his head hung over the back of his chair, but he swings his hands up in the air from time to time to emphasize a point, first one hand and then the other. It looks like he's giving wig-wag signals to the typing pool. The way he hangs himself over the back of the chair—that keeps up the funky shirtsleeve-operation number. And throwing his hands around—that's dy*nam*ic . . . It says, "We're hacking our way through the red tape just as fast as we can."

"Now I'm here to try to answer any questions I can," he says, "but you have to understand that I'm only speaking as an individual, and so naturally none of my comments are binding, but I'll answer any questions I can, and if I can't answer them, I'll do what I can to get the answers for you."

And then it dawns on you, and you wonder why it took so long for you to realize it. This man is the flak catcher. His job is to catch the flak for the No. 1 man. He's like the professional mourners you can hire in Chinatown. They have certified wailers, professional mourners, in Chinatown, and when your loved one dies, you can hire the professional mourners to wail at the funeral and show what a great loss to the community the departed is. In the same way this lifer is ready to catch whatever flak you're sending up. It doesn't matter what bureau they put him in. It's all the same. Poverty, Japanese imports, valley fever, tomato-crop parity, partial disability, home loans, second-probate accounting, the Interstate 90 detour change order, lockouts, secondary boycotts, G.I. alimony, the Pakistani quota, cinch mites, Tularemic Loa loa, veterans' dental benefits, workmen's compensation, suspended excise rebates—whatever you're angry about, it doesn't matter, he's there to catch the flak. He's a lifer.

Everybody knows the scene is a shuck, but you can't just walk out and leave. You can't get it on and bring thirty-five people walking all the way from the Mission to 100 McAllister and then just turn around and go back. So . . . might as well get into the number . . .

One of the Chicanos starts it off by asking the straight question, which is about how many summer jobs the Mission groups are going to get. This is the opening phase, the straight-face phase, in the art of mau-mauing.

"Well," says the Flak Catcher—and he gives it a twist of the head and a fling of the hand and the ingratiating smile—"It's hard for me to answer that the way I'd like to answer it, and the way I know you'd like for me to answer it, because that's precisely what we're working on back in Washington. But I can tell you this. At this point I see no reason why our project allocation should be any less, if all we're looking at is the urban-factor numbers for this area, because that should remain the same. Of course, if there's been any substantial prefunding, in Washington, for the fixed-asset part of our program, like Head Start or the community health centers, that could alter the picture. But we're very hopeful, and as soon as we have the figures, I can tell you that you people will be the first to know."

It goes on like this for a while. He keeps saying things like, "I don't know the answer to that right now, but I'll do everything I can to find out." The way he says it, you can tell he thinks you're going to be impressed with how honest he is about what he doesn't know. Or he says, "I wish we could give *everybody* jobs. Believe me, I would like nothing better, both personally and as a representative of this Office."

So one of the bloods says, "Man, why do you sit there shining us with this bureaucratic rhetoric, when you said yourself that ain't nothing you say that means a goddamn thing?"

Ba-ram-ba-ram-ba-ram-ba-ram—a bunch of the aces start banging on the floor in unison. It sounds like they have sledge hammers.

"Ha-unnnnh," says the Flak Catcher. It is one of those laughs that starts out as a laugh but ends up like he got hit in the stomach halfway through. It's the first assault on his dignity. So he breaks into his shit-eating grin, which is always phase two. Why do so many bureaucrats, deans, preachers, college presidents, try to smile when the mau-mauing starts? It's fatal, this smiling. When some bad dude is challenging your manhood, your smile just proves that he is right and you are chickenshit—unless you are a bad man yourself with so much heart that you can make that smile say, "Just keep on talking, sucker, because I'm gonna count to ten and then *squash* you."

"Well," says the Flak Catcher, "I can't promise you jobs if the jobs aren't available yet"—and then he looks up as if for the first time he is really focusing on the thirty-five ghetto hot dogs he is now facing, by way of sizing up the threat, now that the shit has started. The blacks and the Chicanos he has no doubt seen before, or people just like them, but then he takes in the Filipinos. There are about eight of them, and they are all wearing the Day-Glo yellow and hot-green sweaters and lemon-colored pants and Italian-style socks. But it's the head-gear that does the trick. They've all got on Rap Brown shades and Russian Cossack hats made of frosted-gray Dynel. They look *bad*. Then the man takes in the Samoans, and they look worse. There's about ten of them, but they fill up half the room. They've got on Island shirts with designs in streaks and blooms of red, only it's a really raw shade of red, like that red they paint the floor with in the tool and dye works. They're glaring at him out of those big dark wide brown faces. The monsters have tight curly hair, but it grows in long strands, and they comb it back flat, in long curly strands, with a Duke pomade job. They've got huge feet, and they're wearing san-dals. The straps on the sandals look like they were made from the reins on the Budweiser draft horses. But what really gets the Flak Catcher, besides the sheer size of the brutes, is their Tiki canes. These are like Polynesian scepters. They're the size of sawed-off pool cues, only they're carved all over in Polyne-sian Tiki Village designs. When they wrap their fists around these sticks, every knuckle on their hands pops out the size of a walnut. Anything they hear that they like, like the part about the "bureaucratic rhetoric," they bang on the floor in unison with the ends of the Tiki sticks—*ba-ram-ba-ram-ba-ram-ba-ram*—although some of them press one end of the stick onto the sole of their sandal between their first two toes and raise their foot up and down with the stick to cushion the blow on the floor. They don't want to scuff up the Tiki cane.

The Flak Catcher is still staring at them, and his shit-eating grin is getting worse. It's like he *knows* the worst is yet to come . . . Goddamn . . . that one in front there . . . that Pineapple Brute . . .

"Hey, Brudda," the main man says. He has a really heavy accent. "Hey, Brudda, how much you make?"

"Me?" says the Flak Catcher. "How much do I make?"

"Yeah, Brudda, you. How much money you make?"

Now the man is trying to think in eight directions at once. He tries out a new smile. He tries it out on the bloods, the Chicanos, and the Filipinos, as if to say, "As one intelligent creature to another, what do you do with dumb people like this?" But all he gets is the glares, and his mouth shimmies back into the terrible sickening grin, and then you can see that there are a whole lot of little muscles all around the human mouth, and his are beginning to squirm and tremble . . . He's fighting for control of himself . . . It's a lost cause . . .

"How much, Brudda?"

Ba-ram-ba-ram-ba-ram-ba-ram—they keep beating on the floor.

"Well," says the Flak Catcher, "I make $1,100 a month."

"How come you make so much?"

"Wellllll"—the grin, the last bid for clemency . . . and now the poor man's eyes are freezing into little round iceballs, and his mouth is getting dry—

Ba-ram-ba-ram-ba-ram-ba-ram

"How come you make so much? My fadda and mudda both work and they only make six hundred and fifty."

Oh shit, the cat kind of blew it there. That's way over the poverty line, about double, in fact. It's even above the guideline for a family of twelve. You can see that fact register with the Flak Catcher, and he's trying to work up the nerve to make the devastating comeback. But he's not about to talk back to these giants.

"Listen, Brudda. Why don't you give up your paycheck for summer jobs? You ain't doing shit."

"Wellll"—the Flak Catcher grins, he sweats, he hangs over the back of the chair—

Ba-ram-ba-ram-ba-ram-ba-ram—"Yeah, Brudda! Give us your paycheck!"

There it is . . . the ultimate horror . . . He can see it now, he can hear it . . . Fifteen tons of it . . . It's horrible . . . it's possible . . . It's so obscene, it just might happen . . . Huge Polynesian monsters marching down to his office every payday . . . Hand it over, Brudda . . . ripping it out of his very fingers . . . eternally . . . He wrings his hands . . . the little muscles around his mouth are going haywire. He tries to recapture his grin, but those little amok muscles pull his lips up into an O, like they were drawstrings.

"I'd gladly give up my salary," says the Flak Catcher. "I'd *glad*ly do it, if it would do any good. But can't you see, gentlemen, it would be just a drop in the bucket . . . just a *drop in the bucket*!" This phrase *a drop in the bucket* seems to give him heart . . . it's something to hang onto . . . an answer . . . a reprieve . . . "Just consider what we have to do in this city alone, gentlemen! All of us! It's just a *drop in the bucket*!"

The Samoans can't come up with any answer to this, so the Flak Catcher keeps going.

"Look, gentlemen," he says, "you tell me what to do and I'll do it. Of *course* you want more summer jobs, and we want you to have them. That's what we're here for. I wish I could give everybody a job. You tell me how to get more jobs, and we'll get them. We're doing all we can. If we can do more, you tell me how, and I'll gladly do it."

One of the bloods says, "Man, if you don't *know how,* then we don't *need* you."

"Dat's right, Brudda! Whadda we need you for!" You can tell the Samoans wish they had thought of that shoot-down line themselves—*Ba-ram-ba-ram-ba-ram-ba-ram*—they clobber the hell out of the floor.

"Man," says the blood, "you just taking up space and killing time and drawing pay!"

"Dat's right, Brudda! You just drawing pay!" *Ba-ram-ba-ram-ba-ram-ba-ram*

"Man," says the blood, "if you don't know nothing and you can't do nothing and you can't say nothing, why don't you tell your boss what we want!"

"Dat's right, Brudda! Tell the man!" *Ba-ram-ba-ram-ba-ram-ba-ram*

"As I've already told you, he's in Washington trying to meet the deadlines for *your* projects!"

"You talk to the man, don't you? He'll let you talk to him, won't he?"

"Yes . . ."

"Send him a telegram, man!"

"Well, all right—"

"Shit, pick up the telephone, man!"

"Dat's right, Brudda! Pick up the telephone!" *Ba-ram-ba-ram-ba-ram-ba-ram*

"Please, gentlemen! That's pointless! It's already after six o'clock in Washington. The office is closed!"

"Then call him in the morning, man," says the blood. "We coming back here in the morning and we gonna *watch* you call the man! We gonna stand right on *top* of you so you won't forget to make that call!"

"Dat's right, Brudda! On *top* of you!" *Ba-ram-ba-ram-ba-ram-ba-ram*

"All right, gentlemen . . . all right," says the Flak Catcher. He slaps his hands against his thighs and gets up off the chair. "I'll tell you what . . ." The way he says it, you can tell the man is trying to get back a little corner of his manhood. He tries to take a tone that says, "You haven't really been in here for the past fifteen minutes intimidating me and burying my nuts in the sand and humiliating me . . . We've really been having a discussion about the proper procedures, and I am willing to grant that you have a point."

"If that's what you want," he says, "I'm certainly willing to put in a telephone call."

"If we *want*! If you *willing*! Ain't no want or willing *about* it, man! You *gonna* make that call! We gonna be here and *see* you make it!"

"Dat's right, Brudda! We be seeing you"—*Ba-ram-ba-ram-ba-ram*—"We coming *back*!"

And the Flak Catcher is standing there with his mouth playing bad tricks on him again, and the Samoans hoist their Tiki sticks, and the aces all leave, and they're thinking . . . We've done it again. We've mau-maued the goddamn white man, scared him until he's singing a duet with his sphincter, and the people sure do have power. Did you see the look on his face? Did you see the sucker trembling? Did you see the sucker trying to lick his lips? He was *scared,* man! That's the last time that sucker is gonna try to *urban-factor* and *pre-fund* and *fix-asset* with us! He's gonna go home to his house in Diamond Heights and he's gonna say, "Honey, fix me a drink!

Those motherfuckers were ready to kill me!" That sucker was some kind of *petrified* . . . He could see eight kinds of Tiki sticks up side his head . . .

Of course, the next day nobody shows up at the poverty office to make sure the sucker makes the telephone call. Somehow it always seems to happen that way. Nobody ever follows it up. You can get everything together once, for the demonstration, for the confrontation, to go downtown and maumau, for the fun, for the big show, for the beano, for the main event, to see the people bury some gray cat's nuts and make him crawl and whine and sink in his own terrible grin. But nobody ever follows it up. You just sleep it off until somebody tells you there's going to be another big show.

And then later on you think about it and you say, "What really happened that day? Well, another flak catcher lost his manhood, that's what happened." Hmmmmmm . . . like maybe the bureaucracy isn't so dumb after all . . . All they did was sacrifice one flak catcher, and they've got hundreds, thousands . . . They've got replaceable parts. They threw this sacrifice to you, and you went away pleased with yourself. And even the Flak Catcher himself wasn't losing much. He wasn't losing his manhood. He gave that up a long time ago, the day he became a lifer . . . Just who is fucking over who . . . You did your number and he did his number, and they didn't even have to stop the music . . . The band played on . . . *Still*—did you see the *look* on his face? That sucker—

WHEN BLACK PEOPLE FIRST STARTED USING THE CON-frontation tactic, they made a secret discovery. There was an extra dividend to this tactic. There was a creamy dessert. It wasn't just that you registered your protest and showed the white man that you meant business and weakened his resolve to keep up the walls of oppression. It wasn't just that you got poverty money and influence. There was something sweet that happened right there on the spot. You made the white man quake. You brought *fear* into his face.

Black people began to realize for the first time that the white man, particularly the educated white man, the leadership, had a deep dark Tarzan mumbo jungle voodoo fear of the black man's masculinity. This was a revelation. For two hundred years, wherever black people lived, north or south, mothers had been raising their sons to be meek, to be mild, to check their manhood at the front door in all things that had to do with white people, for fear of incurring the wrath of the Man. The *Man* was the white man. He was the only *man*. And now, when you got him up close and growled, this all-powerful superior animal turned out to be terrified. You could read it in his face. He had the same fear in his face as some good-doing boy who has just moved onto the block and is hiding behind his mama and the moving man and the sofa while the bad dudes on the block size him up.

So for the black man mau-mauing was a beautiful trip. It not only stood to bring you certain practical gains like money and power. It also energized your batteries. It recharged your masculinity. You no longer had to play it cool and go in for pseudo-ignorant malingering and put your head into that Ofay Pig Latin catacomb code style of protest. Mau-mauing brought you respect in its cash forms: namely, fear and envy.

This was the difference between a confrontation and a demonstration. A demonstration, like the civil-rights march on Washington in 1963, could frighten the white leadership, but it was a general fear, an external fear, like being afraid of a hurricane. But in a confrontation, in mau-mauing, the idea was to frighten white men personally, face to face. The idea was to separate the man from all the power and props of his office. Either he had enough heart to deal with the situation or he didn't. It was like saying, "You—yes, you right there on the platform—we're not talking about the *gov*ernment, we're not talking about the *Of*fice of Economic Oppor*tun*ity—we're talking about *you,* you up there with your hands shaking in your pile of papers . . ." If this worked, it created a personal, internal fear. The internal fear was, "I'm afraid I'm not man enough to deal with these bad niggers!"

That may sound like a simple case of black people being good at terrifying whites and whites being quick to run scared. But it was more than that. The strange thing was that the confrontation ritual was built into the poverty program from the beginning. The poverty bureaucrats depended on confrontations in order to know what to do.

Whites were still in the dark about the ghettos. They had been studying the "urban Negro" in every way they could think of for fifteen years, but they found out they didn't know any more about the ghettos than when they started. Every time there was a riot, whites would call on "Negro leaders" to try to cool it, only to find out that the Negro leaders didn't have any followers. They sent Martin Luther King into Chicago and the people ignored him. They sent Dick Gregory into Watts and the people hooted at him and threw beer cans. During the riot in Hunters Point, the mayor of San Francisco, John Shelley, went into Hunters Point with the only black member of the Board of Supervisors, and the brothers threw rocks at both of them. They sent in the middle-class black members of the Human Rights Commission, and the brothers laughed at them and called them Toms. Then they figured the leadership of the riot was "the gangs," so they sent in the "ex–gang leaders" from groups like Youth for Service to make a "liaison with the key gang leaders." What they didn't know was that Hunters Point and a lot of ghettos were so disorganized, there weren't even any "key gangs," much less "key gang leaders," in there. That riot finally just burnt itself out after five days, that was all.

But the idea that the real leadership in the ghetto might be the *gangs* hung on with the poverty-youth-welfare establishment. It was considered a very sophisticated insight. The youth gangs weren't petty criminals . . . they were "social bandits," primitive revolutionaries . . . Of course, they were hidden from public view. That was why the true nature of ghetto leadership had eluded everyone for so long . . . So the poverty professionals were always on the lookout for the bad-acting dudes who were the "real leaders," the "natural leaders," the "charismatic figures" in the ghetto jungle. These were the kind of people the social-welfare professionals in the Kennedy Administration had in mind when they planned the poverty program in the first place. It was a truly adventurous and experimental approach they had. Instead of handing out alms, which never seemed to change anything, they would encourage the people in the ghettos to organize. They would help them become powerful enough to force the Establishment to give them what they needed. From the beginning the poverty program was aimed at helping ghetto people rise up against their oppressors. It was a scene in which the federal government came into the ghetto and said, "Here is some money and some field advisors. Now you organize your own pressure groups." It was no accident that Huey Newton and Bobby

Seale drew up the ten-point program of the Black Panther Party one night in the offices of the North Oakland Poverty Center.

To sell the poverty program, its backers had to give it the protective coloration of "jobs" and "education," the Job Corps and Operation Head Start, things like that, things the country as a whole could accept. "Jobs" and "education" were things everybody could agree on. They were part of the free-enterprise ethic. They weren't uncomfortable subjects like racism and the class structure—and giving the poor the money and the tools to fight City Hall. But from the first that was what the lion's share of the poverty budget went into. It went into "community organizing," which was the bureaucratic term for "power to the people," the term for finding the real leaders of the ghetto and helping them organize the poor.

And how could they find out the identity of these leaders of the people? Simple. In their righteous wrath they would rise up and *confront* you. It was a beautiful piece of circular reasoning. The real leaders of the ghetto will rise up and confront you ... Therefore, when somebody rises up in the ghetto and confronts you, then you know he's a leader of the people. So the poverty program not only encouraged mau-mauing it, it practically *demanded* it. Subconsciously, for administrators in the poverty establishment, public and private, confrontations became a ritual. That was the way the system worked. By 1968 it was standard operating procedure. To get a job in the post office, you filled out forms and took the civil-service exam. To get into the poverty scene, you did some mau-mauing. If you could make the flak catchers lose control of the muscles around their mouths, if you could bring fear into their faces, your application was approved.

NINETY-NINE PERCENT OF THE TIME WHITES WERE IN NO physical danger whatsoever during mau-mauing. The brothers understood through and through that it was a tactic, a procedure, a game. If you actually hurt or endangered somebody at one of these sessions, you were only cutting yourself off from whatever was being handed out, the jobs, the money, the influence. The idea was to terrify but don't touch. The term *mau-mauing* itself expressed this game-like quality. It expressed the put-on side of it. In public you used the same term the whites used, namely, "confrontation." The term *mau-mauing* was a source of amusement in private. The term *mau-mauing* said, "The white man has a voodoo fear of us, because deep down he still thinks we're savages. Right? So we're going to do that Savage number for him." It was like a practical joke at the expense of the white man's superstitiousness.

Almost every time that mau-mauing actually led to violence, you would find a revolutionary core to the organization that was doing it. If an organization was truly committed to revolution, then the poverty program, or the university, or whatever, was only something to hitch a ride on in the first place. Like at San Francisco State when the Black Students Union beat up the editor of the school newspaper, *The Gater,* and roughed up a lot of people during the strike. The BSU was allied with the Black Panthers. Stokely Carmichael, when he was with the Panthers, had come over to State and worked with the BSU, and given a speech that fired up the brothers for action. The willingness to be violent was a way of saying we are serious, we intend to go all the way, this *is* a revolution.

But this was a long way from the notion that all black militants in the ghetto were ready to be violent, to be revolutionaries. They weren't. A lot of whites seemed to think all the angry young men in the ghettos were ready to rise up and follow the Black Panthers at a moment's notice. Actually the Panthers had a complicated status in the ghettos in San Francisco. You talked to almost any young ace on the street, and he admired the Panthers. He looked up to them. The Panthers were stone courageous. They ripped off the white man and blew his mind and fucked him around like nobody has *ev*er done it. And so on. And yet as an organization the Panthers hardly got a toehold in the ghettos in San Francisco, even though their national headquarters were just over the Bay Bridge in Oakland. Whites always seemed to think they had the ghetto's leaders identified and catalogued, and they were always wrong.

Like one time in an English class at San Francisco State there was a teacher who decided to read aloud to the class from *Soul on Ice* by Eldridge Cleaver. This teacher was a white woman. She was one of those Peter, Paul, and Mary–type intellectuals. She didn't wear nylons, she didn't wear make-up, she had bangs and long straight brown hair down to below her shoulders. You see a lot of middle-class white intellectual women like that in California. They have a look that is sort of Pioneer Hip or Salt of the Earth Hip, with flat-heeled shoes and big Honest Calves. Most of the students in her class were middle-class whites. They were the average English literature students. Most of them hadn't even reached the Save the Earth stage, but they dressed Revolutionary Street Fighter. After the strike at State, middle-class students didn't show up on campus any more in letter sweaters or those back-to-school items like you see in the McGregor ads. They dressed righteous and "with the people." They would have on guerrilla gear that was so righteous that Che Guevara would have had to turn in his beret and get bucked down to company chaplain if he had come up against it. They would have on berets and hair down to the shoulders, 1958 Sierra Maestra style, and raggedy field jackets and combat boots and jeans, but not Levi's or Slim Jims or Farahs or Wranglers or any of those tailored hip-hugging jeans, but jeans of the people, the black Can't Bust 'Em brand, hod-carrier jeans that have an emblem on the back of a hairy gorilla, real *funky* jeans, and woolly green socks, the kind that you get at the Army surplus at two pair for twenty-nine cents. Or else they would go for those checked lumberjack shirts that are so heavy and woolly that you can wear them like a jacket. It's like the Revolution has nostalgia for the proletariat of about 1910, the Miners with Dirty Faces era, because today the oppressed, the hard-core youth in the ghetto—they aren't into the Can't Bust 'Ems with the gorilla and the Army surplus socks. They're into the James Brown look. They're into the ruffled shirts, the black belted leather pieces from Boyd's on Market Street, the bell-cuff herringbones, all that stuff, looking sharp. If you tried to put one of those lumpy lumberjack shirts on them, they'd vomit. Anyway, most of the students in this woman's English literature class were white middle class, but there were two or three students from the ghettos.

She starts reading aloud from *Soul on Ice,* and she's deep into it. She's got the whole class into Eldridge Cleaver's cell-block in San Quentin, and Cleaver is telling about his spiritual awakening and how he discovered the important revolutionary thinkers. She goes on and on, a long passage, and she has a pure serene tone going. When she finishes, she looks up in the most soulful way, with her chin up and her eyes shining, and she closes the book very softly under her chin, the way a preacher closes the Bible.

Naturally all of the white kids are wiped out. They're sitting there looking at each other and saying, "Far out" . . . "Too much" . . . "Wow, that's heavy" . . . They're shaking their heads and looking very solemn. It's obvious that they just assume that Eldridge Cleaver speaks for all the black people and that what we need is a revolution . . . That's the only thing that will change this rotten system . . . In their minds they're now in the San Francisco State cellblock, and the only thing that is going to alter this shit is the Big Bust-out . . .

The teacher lets all this sink in, and then she says: "I'd like to hear some comments."

One of the ghetto brothers raises his hand, and she turns to him with the most radiant brotherly smile the human mind can imagine and says, "Yes?"

And this student, a funky character with electric hair, says: "You know what? Ghetto people would laugh if they heard what you just read. That book wasn't written for the ghettos. It was written for the white middle class. They published it and they read it. What is this 'having previously dabbled in the themes and writings of Rousseau, Thomas Paine, and Voltaire' that he's laying down in there? You try coming down in the Fillmore doing some *previously dabbling* and talking about Albert Camus and James Baldwin. They'd laugh you off the block. That book was written to give a thrill to white women in Palo Alto and Marin County. That book is the best su*burb*an jive I ever heard. I don't think he even wrote it. Eldridge Cleaver wouldn't write something like that. I think his wife wrote it . . . *Pre-vi-ously dab-bled* . . . I mean like don't dabble the people no previouslies and don't previous the people no dabblies and don't preevy-dabble the people with no split-level Palo Alto white bourgeois housewife Buick Estate Wagon backseat rape fantasies . . . you know? . . ."

As you can see, the man goes completely off his bean on this subject. He's saying every outrageous thing that bubbles up into his brain, because he wants to blow the minds of the whites in the room. They're all staring at him with congealed faces, like they just got sapped in the back of the neck. They hardly had a chance to get down into the creamy pudding of their romantic Black Hero trip, when this dude comes along and unloads on them. But they don't dare say a word against him, because he's hard-core, and he has that ghetto patter. He's the one who must know . . .

So mostly the fellow is trying to blow their minds because they are being so smug and knowing about The Black Man. He's saying, Don't try to tell *us* who our leaders are, because you don't know. And that's the truth. The Panthers were righteous brothers, but there were a lot of militants in the ghettos of San Francisco who had their own numbers going. There were the Mission Rebels, the Cortland Progressives, the New Society, the United Council for Black Dignity, the Young Adults, the New Thang, the Young Men for Action . . . it was a list with no end . . . By the time you completed a list of all the organizations that existed at any given time, some new ones would have already started . . . Everybody had his own angle and his own way of looking at black power. The Panthers were on a very special trip. The Panthers were fighting the Pig. And the Pig was fighting the Panthers. If you joined the Panthers, you had to be ready to fight the police, because that was the trip you'd be on. One of the main things you stood to get out of it was a club up side your head, or a bullet. If you were a man who had really been worked over by the police, then you could relate to that and you were ready for that fight. The Panthers were like the Muslims in that respect. But as bad as things were in the ghettos, there weren't but so many aces who were ready to play it all-or-nothing that way.

The ghettos were full of "individualists" . . . in the sense the Russian revolutionaries used to use that word about the lumpenproletariat of Russia. The lumpenproletariat—the "underclass," as they say today—used to drive the Russian revolutionaries up the wall. Someone like Nikolai Bukharin would end up talking about them like he was some cracker judge from the year 1911: ". . . shiftlessness, lack of discipline, hatred of the old, but impotence to construct or organize anything new, an individualistic declassed 'personality,' whose actions are based only on foolish caprices . . ." He sounded like some Grand Kloogle on the bedsheet circuit.

In the ghettos the brothers grew up with their own outlook, their own status system. Near the top of the heap was the pimp style. In all the commission reports and studies and syllabuses you won't see anything about the pimp style. And yet there it was. In areas like Hunters Point boys didn't grow up looking up to the man who had a solid job working for some company or for the city, because there weren't enough people who had such jobs. It seemed like nobody was going to make it *by* working, so the king was the man who made out best by *not* working, by *not* sitting all day under the Man's bitch box. And on the street the king was the pimp. Sixty years ago Thorstein Veblen wrote that at the very bottom of the class system, down below the "working class" and the "honest poor," there was a "spurious aristocracy," a leisure class of bottom dogs devoted to luxury and aristocratic poses. And there you have him, the

pimp. The pimp is the dude who wears the $150 Sly
Stone–style vest and pants outfit from the haberdasheries on
Polk and the $35 Lester Chambers–style four-inch-brim black
beaver fedora and the thin nylon socks with the vertical stripes
and drives the customized sun-roof Eldorado with the Jaguar
radiator cap. The pimp was the aristocrat of the street hustle.
But there were other lines of work that the "spurious aristocrats" might be into. They might be into gambling, dealing
drugs, dealing in stolen goods or almost anything else. They
would truck around in the pimp style, too. Everything was the
street hustle. When a boy was growing up, it might take the
form of getting into gangs or into a crowd that used drugs.
There were plenty of good-doing boys who grew up under the
shadows of their mothers and were aiming toward a straight
life. But they were out of it in their own community. The status system on the block would be running against them, and
they wouldn't "come out," meaning come out of the house and
be on their own, until their late teens.

The pimp style was a supercool style that was much admired or envied. You would see some dude, just some brother
from down the hall, walking down the street with his Rollo
shirt on, and his black worsted bells with a three-button fly at
the bell bottom of each pants leg, giving a spats effect, and he
is walking with that rolling gait like he's got a set of ball-
bearing discs in his shoulders and his hips, and you can say to
the dude, "Hey, Pimp!" and he's not offended. He'll chuckle
and say, "How you doing, baby." He's smiling and pleased
with himself, because you're pulling his leg but at the same
time you're saying that he's looking cool, looking sharp, looking good.

Sometimes a group of buddies who ran together, who were

"stone pimp," as the phrase went, would move straight into the poverty program. They would do some fabulous, awesome, inspired mau-mauing, and the first thing you knew, they would be hanging out in the poverty scene. The middle-class bureaucrats, black and white, would never know what to make of an organization like this. They couldn't figure them out. There was one organization in a city just outside of San Francisco, in the kind of section that catches the bums, the winos, the prostitutes with the biscuits & gravy skin, the gay boys, the flaming lulus, the bike riders, the porno shops, peep shows, $8-a-week hotels with the ripped window shades flapping out. This area had everything you needed for a successful application for a poverty-program grant except for the one thing you need the most, namely, the militant youth. So that was when a remarkable ace known as Dudley showed up with a couple of dozen bonafide spurious aristocrats . . . his Ethnic Catering Service for skid row . . . There wasn't one of them that looked much under thirty, and nobody had ever heard of any black youth in that area before anyway, but they could mau-mau as if they had been trained by the great Chaser himself . . . They got a grant of nearly $100,000.

Every now and then the poverty bureaucrats from the Economic Opportunity Council or from City Hall would hold an area executive board meeting or some other kind of session at their clubhouse, and it was always a bear. A group of poverty workers and administrators would walk in there for the first time, and you could tell from the looks on their faces that something had hit them as different . . . and weird . . . They *felt* it . . . they *sensed* it . . . without knowing what it was. Actually it was a simple thing. The pimp-style aristocrats would be sitting around like a bunch of secretary birds.

There would be Dudley and the boys . . . Dudley, with his Fuzzy-Wuzzy natural and his welts. Dudley was a powerful man with big slabs of muscle like Sonny Liston and these long welts, like the welted seams on top of a pair of moccasins, on his cheeks, his neck, on the backs of his fists. These welts were like a historical map of fifteen years of Saturday night knife-fighting in the Bay Area. And Dudley's Afro . . . the brother had grown the rankest natural of all times. It wasn't shaped or anything close to it. It was growing like a clump of rumpus weed by the side of the road. It was growing every which way, and it wasn't even all one color. There was a lot of gray in it. It looked superfunky. It looked like he'd taken the stuffing out of the seat of one of those old ripped-up chairs you see out on the sidewalk with its insides spilling out after a fire on Webster Street—it looked like he'd taken the stuffing out of one of those chairs and packed it all over his head. Dudley was the fiercest looking man in the Bay Area, but there would be him and all his boys sitting around like a covey of secretary birds.

That was the pimp look, the look of hip and supercool and so fine. The white bureaucrats, and the black ones, too, walked in trying to look as earthy and rugged as they could, in order to be "with the people." They tried to walk in like football players, like they had a keg of beer between their legs. They rounded their shoulders over so it made their necks look bigger. They thickened up their voices and threw a few "mans" and "likes" and "digs" into their conversations. When they sat down, they gave it that Honcho wide-open spread when they crossed their legs, putting the right foot, encased in a cordovan brogue with a sole sticking out like a rock ledge, on the left knee, as if the muscles in their thighs were so big and stud-like that they couldn't cross their legs all the way if they tried. But the pimp-style aristocrats had taken the manhood thing through so many numbers that it was beginning to come out through the other side. To them, by now, being hip was striking poses that were so cool, so languid, they were almost feminine. It was like saying, "We've got masculinity to spare." We've been through so much shit, we're so confident of our manhood, we're so hip and so suave and wise in the ways of the street, that we can afford to be re*fined* and not sit around here trying to look like a bunch of stud brawlers. So they would not only cross their legs, they'd cross them further than a woman would. They would cross them so far, it looked like one leg was wrapped around the other one three or four times. One leg would seem to wrap around the other one and disappear in the back of the knee socket. And they'd be leaning forward in the chair with their heads cocked to one side and their chins hooked over their collarbones and their shades riding low on their noses, and they'd be peering out over the upper rim of the shades. And they'd have one hand cocked in front of their chins, hanging limp at the wrist with the forefinger sticking out like some kind of curved beak. They would look like one of those supercool secretary birds that stand around on one long A-1 racer leg with everything else drawn up into a beautiful supercool little bunch of fluffy feathers at the top.

They liked to run a meeting like everything else, namely, very cool. Dudley was conducting the meeting when in through the back door comes one of his boys, a tall dude with the cool rolling gait and his hands stuck in his pants pockets, which are the high Western-style pockets. The door he came in leads up a short flight of stairs and out onto an alley. This is a commercial district, and the alley is one of those dead-end slits they use for deliveries. It's always full of corrugated boxes and excelsior and baling wire and industrial wrapping paper and other debris. It's the kind of alley that has a little half sidewalk on one side and there are always a couple of cars parked lopsided with two wheels up on the sidewalk and two on the alley. Anyway, the dude comes lollygagging in, as cool as you please, and walks over to where Dudley is sitting like a secretary bird and leans over and whispers something to him. Even the way he leans over is stone pimp-style. His legs don't bend and his back doesn't bend. It's like he's been cleaned, pressed, and Perma-creased at hip level, right where his hand fits into his Western pocket, and he just jackknifes at the desired angle where the crease is. He keeps his hand in the pocket when he bends over. He just lets the hand bend backward at the wrist. It looks like his fingers are caught in his appendix.

"Say *what,* man?" says Dudley. "Don't you see I'm trying to hold a con-fer-ence in here?"

"But like man," says the Dude, "this is ve-ry im-por-tant."

"What the hell you into that's so im-por-tant, sucker?"

"Well, man, just wait a *min*-ute and let me tell you. You know that wino, Half and Half, that hangs out in the alley?"

"Yeah, I know him."

"Well, man, he's out there in the alley trying to burn down the buil-ding."

Dudley doesn't even move at first. He just peers out over his shades at his boys and at all the bureaucrats from downtown, and then he cocks his head and cocks his index finger in front of his chin and says, "We gonna have a tem-po-rary re-cess. The brother ask me to take care some business."

Then Dudley unwinds very casually and stands up, and he and the brother start walking toward the back door, but so cool and so slow, with the whole rolling gait, that it looks like

Marcel Marceau doing one of those walks where he doesn't actually move off the spot he started on. They open the door like they're going out to check out the weather, but once they're on the other side—*whoosh!*—it's like somebody lit their afterburners. They're up those stairs like a rocket and out into the alley and on top of the wino, Half and Half, in just under one half a second.

This Half and Half is one of those stone winos who hang around there, one of those winos whose face is so weatherbeaten it looks like a pebble-grain full-brogue oxblood shoe. He has white hair, but a full head of white hair, so thick it looks like every hair he ever had in his head was nailed in for good. All that boozing and drinking half-and-half, which is half sherry and half port, must do righteous things for the hair, because there are no old men in the world who have hair like the winos. This Half and Half is such a stone wino that the only clothes he has left are the green KP fatigues they hand out in the hospitals and the jails, because the rest have been ripped up, vomited on, or stolen. He has on the fatigues and a pair of black street shoes with thin white hospital socks. He has pushed the socks way down into the heels of the shoes because his ankles are swollen and covered with skin ulcers, which he swabs with paper towels he cops from out of the public toilets. The old crock hates these black studs who have turned up down on his skid-row cul-de-sac, and he keeps trying to burn up the building. He has a big pile of paper and excelsior and other stuff shoved up against the wall and he has it smoldering in a kind of fogged-in wino way, trying to in-cin-e-rate the mother.

All of that is going on outside in the alley. From inside the clubhouse at first there's nothing: silence. Then you start to hear a sound that sounds like there is a paddlewheel from off

a Mississippi steamboat out there in the alley, and to every pad-
dle is attached a size 12E motorcycle boot, and as the wheel
goes around every one of these boots hits the wino...
thunk...*thunk*...*whop*...*whump*...*thunk*...*thunk*...
whop...*whump*...

The white bureaucrats and the black bureaucrats look at
Dudley's boys, and Dudley's boys just stare back over the top
of their shades and sit there wound and cocked as coolly as the
secretary bird...

thunk...*thunk*...*whop*...*whump*...*thunk*...*thunk*...
whop...*whump*...

And then the white bureaucrats look at the black bureaucrats and the black bureaucrats look at the white bureaucrats,
and one of the bureaucrats who is dressed in the Roos-Atkins
Ivy League clothes and the cordovan shoes starts going "Unh,
unh, unh." The thing is, the man thinks he doesn't have any
more middle-class Uncle Tom mannerisms and attributes, but
he just can't help going into that old preachery "Unh, unh,
unh."

thunk...*thunk*...*whop*...*whump*...
"Unh, unh, unh."
thunk...*thunk*...*whop*...*whump*...
"Unh, unh, unh."

Then it stops and the door opens again, and Dudley and the
Dude come walking back in even slower and more cool except
for the fact that they're breathing hard, and they take their
seats and cross their legs and get wound back up and cocked
and perched, and Dudley peers out over his shades and says,
"The meeting is resumed."

BROTHERS FROM DOWN THE HALL LIKE DUDLEY GOT DOWN
to the heart of the poverty program very rapidly. It took them
no time at all to see that the poverty program's big projects,
like manpower training, in which you would get some job
counseling and some training so you would be able to apply
for a job in the bank or on the assembly line—everybody with
a brain in his head knew that this was the usual bureaucratic
shuck. Eventually the government's own statistics bore out the
truth of this conclusion. The ghetto youth who completed the
manpower training didn't get any more jobs or earn any more
money than the people who never took any such training at
all. Everybody but the most hopeless lames knew that the only
job you wanted out of the poverty program was a job *in* the
program itself. Get on the payroll, that was the idea. Never
mind *getting* some job counseling. *You* be the job counselor.
You be the "neighborhood organizer." As a job counselor or a
neighborhood organizer you stood to make six or seven hundred dollars a month, and you were still your own man. Like
if you were a "neighborhood organizer," all you had to do was
go out and get the names and addresses of people in the ghetto
who wanted to relate to the services of the poverty center. That
was a very flexible arrangement. You were still on the street,
and you got paid for it. You could still run with the same buddies you always ran with. There was nobody looking over
your shoulder. You didn't have to act like a convert, like the
wino who has to sing hymns at the mission before he can get
his dinner, to get something out of the poverty scene. In fact,
the more outrageous you were, the better. That was the only
way they knew you were a real leader. It was true that middle-
class people who happened to live in the target areas got the
top jobs, but there was still room for street types.

You'd run into some ace on the corner and you'd say, "Hey, man, what you doing?"

And he'd say, "Nothing, man, what you doing?"

And you'd say, "I'm a neighborhood organizer," or "I'm a job counselor, man" . . . and that gave you status, because it was well known that there were some righteous brothers in on the poverty program.

Some of the main heroes in the ghetto, on a par with the Panthers even, were the Blackstone Rangers in Chicago. The Rangers were so bad, the Rangers so terrified the whole youth welfare poverty establishment, that in one year, 1968, they got a $937,000 grant from the Office of Economic Opportunity in Washington. The Ranger leaders became job counselors in the manpower training project, even though most of them never had a job before and weren't about to be looking for one. This wasn't a case of the Blackstone Rangers putting some huge prank over on the poverty bureaucrats, however. It was in keeping with the poverty program's principle of trying to work through the "real leaders" of the black community. And if they had to give it the protective coloration of "manpower training," then that was the way it would have to be done. Certainly there was no one who could doubt that the Blackstone Rangers were the most powerful group in the Woodlawn area of Chicago. They had the whole place terrified. The Rangers were too much. They were champions. In San Francisco the champions were the Mission Rebels. The Rebels got every kind of grant you could think of, from the government, the foundations, the churches, individual sugar daddies, from everywhere, plus a headquarters building and poverty jobs all over the place.

The police would argue that in giving all that money to

gangs like the Blackstone Rangers the poverty bureaucrats were financing criminal elements and helping to destroy the community. The poverty bureaucrats would argue that they were doing just the opposite. They were bringing the gangs into the system. Back in 1911 Robert Michels, a German sociologist, wrote that the bureaucracy provides the state with a great technique for self-preservation. The bureaucracy has the instinct to expand in any direction. The bureaucracy has the instinct to get all the discontented elements of the society involved and entangled in the bureaucracy itself. In the late 1960's it looked like he might be right. By the end of 1968 there were no more gangs in San Francisco in the old sense of the "fighting gangs." Everybody was into black power, brown power, yellow power, and the poverty program in one way or another. This didn't mean that crime decreased or that a man discontinued his particular hustles. But it did mean he had a different feeling about himself. He wasn't a hustler or a hood. He was a fighter for the people, a ghetto warrior. In the long run it may turn out that the greatest impact of the poverty program, like some of the WPA projects of the Depression, was not on poverty but on morale, on the status system on the streets. Some day the government may look back and wish it had given the Flak Catchers Distinguished Service medals, like the astronauts.

The poverty program, the confrontations, the mau-mauing, brought some of the talented aces something more. It brought them celebrity, overnight. You'd turn on the TV, and there would be some dude you had last seen just hanging out on the corner with the porkpie hat scrunched down over his eyes and the toothpick nodding on his lips—and there he was now on the screen, a leader, a "black spokesman," with whites in the round-shouldered suits and striped neckties holding microphones up to his mouth and waiting for The Word to fall from his lips.

BUT WHATEVER YOU WANTED TO ACHIEVE, FOR YOUR PEOple, for the community, or for yourself and your buddies—the competition was getting rough. Every day there were new organizations coming out of the woodwork. To get your organization in on the poverty program, you had to get recognized by some official agency, and to get recognized you had to do some mau-mauing in most cases. Once you got recognition, then you had the bureaucrats working full-time for you, drawing up the statistics and prospectuses, knocking on the right doors, and making the applications for the "funding," the money that was available from the government, the foundations, or the churches.

But it didn't end there. Just like you were trying to put the pressure on the bureaucrats, the brothers in your organization would be putting the pressure on you. They'd be waiting on your doorstep to see if you were getting anything for the brothers, to see if you really had any class. That was one reason why Summer Jobs was such a big deal. That was what the whole session between the Samoans and the Flak Catcher was over, summer jobs. The jobs themselves were nothing. They were supposed to be for teenagers from poor families. It was an O.E.O. program, and you got $1.35 an hour and ended up as a file clerk or stock-room boy in some federal office or some foundation—hell, they didn't even need one half the people they already had working for them, and so all you learned was how to make work, fake work, and malinger out by the Xerox machine. It is true that you learned those skills from experts in the field, but it was a depressing field to be in.

Nevertheless, there was some fierce mau-mauing that went on over summer jobs, especially in 1969, when the O.E.O. started cutting back funds and the squeeze was on. Half of it was sheer status. There were supposed to be strict impartial guidelines determining who got the summer jobs—but the plain fact was that half the jobs were handed out organization by organization, according to how heavy your organization was. If you could get twenty summer jobs for your organization, when the next organization only got five, then you were four times the aces they were ... no lie ... But there were so many groups out mau-mauing, it was hard to make yourself heard over the uproar. You practically had to stand in line. It was a situation that called for a show of class. You had to show some style, some imagination, some ingenuity.

It brought out the genius in seemingly plain people. Like there was one man with a kind of common name like Bill Jackson. He and some of his buddies had created a poverty organization, the Youth of the Future, and had gotten recognition from one of the E.O.C. area boards. But when it came to summer jobs, the Youth of the Future was out of it, like a lot of organizations. Apparently some people thought that was all the Youth of the Future was, just another organization on the poverty scene, just this Bill Jackson and his buddies from off the block.

So one morning about eleven o'clock a flamboyant black man in a dashiki turns up at City Hall. And this flamboyant black man, the Dashiki Chieftain, isn't running with any brothers from off the block. He is at the head of an army of about sixty young boys and girls from the ghetto. And even his dashiki—it's no ordinary dashiki. This number is *elegant*. It's made of the creamiest black and red wool with great leopard-fur cuffs on the sleeves and leopard-fur patch pockets on the front . . . and a belt. You don't see a dashiki with a belt every day. And he has one of those leopard-fur African fez numbers on his head, and around his neck he has a necklace with beads and tiger teeth leading down to a kind of African carved head pendant. He comes marching up the stairs of City Hall and through those golden doors in his Somaliland dashiki, leading the children's army. And these kids are not marching in any kind of formation, either. They are swinging very free, with high spirits and good voices. The Dashiki Chief has distributed among them all the greatest grandest sweetest creamiest runniest and most luscious mess of All-American pop drinks, sweets, and fried food ever brought together in one place. Sixty strong, sixty loud, sixty wild, they come swinging into the great plush gold-and-marble lobby of the San Francisco City Hall with their hot dogs, tacos, Whammies, Frostees, Fudgsicles, french fries, Eskimo Pies, Awful-Awfuls, Sugar-Daddies, Sugar-Mommies, Sugar-Babies, chocolate-covered frozen bananas, malted milks, Yoo-Hoos, berry pies, bubble gums, cotton candy, Space Food sticks, Frescas, Baskin-Robbins boysenberry-cheesecake ice-cream cones, Milky Ways, M&Ms, Tootsie Pops, Slurpees, Drumsticks, jelly doughnuts, taffy apples, buttered Karamel Korn, root-beer floats, Hi-C punches, large Cokes, 7UPs, 3 Musketeer bars, frozen Kool-Aids—with the Dashiki Chief in the vanguard.

In no time at all the man's dashiki is practically flapping in the breeze from the hurricane of little bodies swirling around him, roaring about with their creamy wavy gravy food and drink held up in the air like the torches of freedom, pitching and rolling at the most perilous angles, a billow of root-beer float here . . . a Yoo-Hoo typhoon there . . . The kids have discovered the glories of the City Hall lobby. Such echoes! Their voices ricochet off the marble in the most groovy way. Screams work best, screams and great hollow shrieks . . . and the most high-toned clatter of sixty pairs of little feet running at top speed . . . This place is Heaven off-the-rack!

The lobby is officially known as the great central court, and it's like some Central American opera house: marble, arches, domes, acanthus leaves and Indian sandstone, quirks and galleries, and gilt filigrees, like Bourbon Louis curlicues of gold in every corner, along every molding, every flute, every cusp, every water-leaf and cartouche, a veritable angels' choir of gold, a veritable obsession of gold . . . and all kept polished as if for the commemoration of the Generalissimo's birthday . . . and busts of great and glorious mayors of San Francisco, perched on top of pedestals in their business suits with their bald marble skulls reflecting the lacy gold of the place . . . Angelo Rossi . . . James Rolph . . . cenotaphs, pediments, baroque balusters, and everywhere marble, marble, marble, gold, gold, gold . . . and through this Golden Whore's Dream of Paradise rush the children of the Youth of the Future.

By now the guards are asking the Dashiki Chief what he thinks he's doing. City Hall functionaries are asking him what he wants. The Dashiki Chief informs them that his name is Jomo Yarumba, and the Youth of the Future are now here, and he wants to see Mayor Joseph Alioto.

Meanwhile, the childstorm is intensifying. A little girl carrying a soft-top beer-style container of Fresca is about to collide with a little boy holding a double-dip Baskin-Robbins strawberry rhubarb sherbet cone, and the City Hall lifers can envision it already: a liver-red blob of sherbet sailing over the marble expanse of the City Hall lobby on a foaming bile-green sea of Fresca, and the kids who are trying to rip the damned paper off the ice cream in the Drumstick popsicles, which always end up inextricable messes of crabbed paper and molten milk fat, mixing it up with the kids whose frozen Kool-Aids are leaking horrible streaks of fuchsia and tubercular blue into the napkins they have wrapped around them in their palms and mashing it all onto the marble bean of Mayor Angelo Rossi . . . and now Jomo Yarumba and his childstorm are swooping up the great marble stairs of the great central court toward the first gallery and the outer office of the Mayor himself, and the City Hall functionaries are beginning to confer in alarm. By and by a young man from the Mayor's office comes out and explains to Jomo Yarumba that the Mayor regrets he has a very tight schedule today and can't possibly see him.

"We'll wait for the cat to get through," says the Dashiki Chief.

"But he's completely tied up, all day."

"Hell, man, we'll stay here all night. We'll see the cat in the morning."

"All night?"

"That's right. We ain't budging, man. We're here to tend to business."

The young guy from the Mayor's office retreats . . . Much consternation and concern in the lobby of City Hall . . . the hurricane could get worse. The little devils could start screaming, wailing, ululating, belching, moaning, giggling, making spook-show sounds . . . filling the very air with a hurricane of malted milk, an orange blizzard of crushed ice from the

Slurpees, with acid red horrors like the red from the taffy apples and the jelly from the jelly doughnuts, with globs of ice cream in purple sheets of root beer, with plastic straws and huge bilious waxed cups and punch cans and sprinkles of Winkles, with mustard from off the hot dogs and little lettuce shreds from off the tacos, with things that splash and things that plop and things that ooze and stick, that filthy sugar moss from off the cotton candy, and the Karamel Korn and the butterscotch daddy figures from off the Sugar-Daddies and the butterscotch babies from off the Sugar-Babies, sugar, water, goo, fried fat, droplets, driplets, shreds, bits, lumps, gums, gobs, smears, from the most itchy molecular Winkle to the most warm moist emetic mass of 3 Musketeers bar and every gradation of solubility and liquidity known to syrup—filling the air, choking it, getting trapped gurgling and spluttering in every glottis—

And it was here that Bill Jackson proved himself to be a brilliant man and a true artist, a rare artist, of the mau-mau. One of the few things that could stir every bureaucrat in City Hall, make every bureaucrat rev up his adrenaline and quicken his pulse and cut the red tape and bypass the normal channels and get it together by word of mouth, by jungle drum, by hoot and holler from floor to floor, was just what Bill Jackson was doing now. Even an armed attack wouldn't have done so much. There's already an 84-page contingency paper for armed attack, emergency guidelines, action memos, with all the channels laid down in black and white for bucking the news up the chain . . . But this! Sixty black hellions and some kind of crazy in a dashiki wreaking creamy wavy gravy through the grand central court of City Hall . . . This lacerated the soul of every lifer, every line bureaucrat, every flak catcher in the municipal government . . . There are those who may think that the bureaucrats and functionaries of City Hall are merely time servers, with no other lookout than filling out their forms, drawing their pay, keeping the boat from rocking and dreaming of their pension like the lid on an orderly life. But bureaucrats, especially in City Halls, have a hidden heart, a hidden well of joy, a low-dosage euphoria that courses through their bodies like thyroxin . . . Because they have a secret: each, in his own way, is hooked into The Power. The Government is The Power, and they are the Government, and the symbol of the Government is the golden dome of City Hall, and the greatest glory of City Hall is the gold-and-marble lobby, gleaming and serene, cool and massive, studded with the glistening busts of bald-headed men now as anonymous as themselves but touched and blessed forever by The Power . . . And in an age of torrid sensations, of lust, gluttony, stroke-house movies, fellatio-lipped young buds jiggling down the street with their hard little nipples doing the new boogaloo through their translucent nylon jerseys, an age of marijuana, LSD, TCH, MDA, cocaine, methedrine, and motels where the acrid electric ozone of the central air conditioning mixes with the sickly sweet secretions oozing from every aperture—in the midst of such cheap thrills and vibrating nerve ends, who is left to record the secret, tender, subtle, and ineffable joys of the line bureaucrat savoring the satin cushion of City Hall? Who else is left to understand the secret bliss of the coffee break at 10:30 a.m., the walk with one's fellows through the majesty of the gold-and-marble lobby and out across the grass and the great white walkways of City Hall Plaza, past the Ionic columns and Italian Renaissance façade of the Public Library on the opposite side and down McAllis-

ter Street a few steps to the cafeteria, where you say hello to
Jerry as he flips the white enamel handle on the urn and pours
you a smoking china mug of coffee and you sit down at a
Formica table and let coffee and cigarette smoke seep through
you amid the Spanish burble of the bus boys, knowing that it
is all set and cushioned, solid and yet lined with velvet, all
waiting for you, as long as you want it, somewhere below your
consciousness, the Bourbon Louis baroque hulk and the
golden dome of City Hall, waiting for you on the walk back,
through the Plaza and up the steps and into the great central
court, and you stop and talk with your good buddy by the door
to the Registrar's or by the bust of Mayor Angelo Rossi, both
of you in your shirtsleeves but with your ties held down
smoothly by a small-bar tie clip, rocking back on the heels of
your Hush Puppies, talking with an insider's chuckles of how
that crazy messenger, the one with the glass eye, got caught
trying to run football-pool cards off on the Xerox machine because he couldn't see the Viper standing there on his blind side
for five minutes with his arms folded, just watching him . . .
while your eyes play over the lobby and all the hopeless wondering mendicants who wander in off the street, looking this
way and that for some sign of where the Assessor's office is, or
the Board of Supervisors', or the Tax Collector's, probably taking their first plunge into the endless intricate mysteries of
The Power, which they no more understand than they could
understand the comradely majesty of this place, this temple,
this nave and crossing of the euphoria of The Power—and
suddenly here are these black ragamuffins! neither timorous
nor bewildered! On the contrary—sportive, scornful, berserk,
filling the air, the very sanctum, with far-flung creamy wavy
gravy, with their noise, their insolence, their pagan vulgarity

and other shitfire and abuse! And no one can lay a hand on them! No one can call in the Tac Squad to disperse sixty black children having a cotton-candy and M&M riot for themselves ... The infidels are immune ...

The incredible news was now sweeping through City Hall. The Mayor's number-three man came out and took a look and disappeared. The Mayor's number-two man came out and took a look and disappeared. The Mayor's press secretary came out and took a look ... it was rumored that The Media were heading over ... and the press secretary disappeared, and the kids dervished through it all, spinning their inspired typhoon up to the very architraves, and Bill Jackson orchestrated the madness in his whirling dashiki ...

And in no time at all here was the Man himself, Mayor Joseph Alioto, advancing into their midst, attended by the number-four man, the number-three man, the number-two man, and the press secretary, and with his bald head gleaming as gloriously as Angelo Rossi's or James Rolph's, heading toward Jomo Yarumba with his broad smile beaming as if he had known the famous youth leader all his life, as if nothing in the world had been weighing more on his mind this morning than getting downstairs promptly to meet the inspiring Youth of the Future ... And as the Mayor shook hands with Jomo Yarumba—there! it was done in a flash!—the Youth of the Future were now home safe ...

Thereafter Bill Jackson could get down to the serious business, which was to use his official recognition to raise money for the sewing machines for his organization's dashiki factory ... black-designed, black-made, black-worn dashikis to be manufactured by the youth themselves ... There were no two ways about it. Bill Jackson and his group were looking good. That particular scene gave a lot of people heart. It wasn't long before an enterprising brother named Ronnie started his own group, The New Thang.

"The New *Thang*?" said Mayor Alioto, after they had put in their own unique and confounding appearance at City Hall.

"That's right, The New Thang."

The Mayor looked wigged out, as if the lights had gone out in his skull.

"Thang," said Ronnie. "That's Thing in African."

"Oh," said the Mayor. There wasn't even the faintest shade of meaning in his voice.

THE PAINTED WORD

The Painted Word

PEOPLE DON'T READ THE MORNING NEWSPAPER, MAR-
shall McLuhan once said, they slip into it like a warm
bath. Too true, Marshall! Imagine being in New York
City on the morning of Sunday, April 28, 1974, like I
was, slipping into that great public bath, that vat, that
spa, that regional physiotherapy tank, that White Sul-
phur Springs, that Marienbad, that Ganges, that River
Jordan for a million souls which is the Sunday *New
York Times*. Soon I was submerged, weightless, suspended in the tepid depths of the thing, in Arts &
Leisure, Section 2, page 19, in a state of perfect sensory
deprivation, when all at once an extraordinary thing
happened:

I *noticed something!*

Yet another clam-broth-colored current had begun

to roll over me, as warm and predictable as the Gulf Stream . . . a review, it was, by the *Times*'s dean of the arts, Hilton Kramer, of an exhibition at Yale University of "Seven Realists," seven realistic painters . . . when I was *jerked alert* by the following:

"Realism does not lack its partisans, but it does rather conspicuously lack a persuasive theory. And given the nature of our intellectual commerce with works of art, to lack a persuasive theory is to lack something crucial—the means by which our experience of individual works is joined to our understanding of the values they signify."

Now, you may say, My God, man! You woke up over *that*? You forsook your blissful coma over a mere swell in the sea of words?

But I knew what I was looking at. I realized that without making the slightest effort I had come upon one of those utterances in search of which psychoanalysts and State Department monitors of the Moscow or Belgrade press are willing to endure a lifetime of tedium: namely, the seemingly innocuous *obiter dicta,* the words in passing, that give the game away.

What I saw before me was the critic-in-chief of *The New York Times* saying: In looking at a painting today, "to lack a persuasive theory is to lack something crucial." I read it again. It didn't say "something helpful" or "enriching" or even "extremely valuable." No, the word was *crucial*.

In short: frankly, these days, without a theory to go with it, I can't see a painting.

Then and there I experienced a flash known as the *Aha!* phenomenon, and the buried life of contemporary art was revealed to me for the first time. The fogs lifted! The clouds passed! The motes, scales, conjunctival bloodshots, and Murine agonies fell away!

All these years, along with countless kindred souls, I am certain, I had made my way into the galleries of Up-

Courtesy Museum of Fine Arts, Boston

Jean François Millet, *The Sower* (1850–51).

At the time Millet was considered something of a rip, because he painted such Low Rent folk. Only later was this called "literary" or "narrative" art per Madison and Lower Soho and the Art Gildo Midway of Fifty-seventh Street, and into the museums, into the Modern, the Whitney, and the Guggenheim, the Bastard Bauhaus, the New Brutalist, and the Fountainhead Baroque, into the lowliest storefront churches and grandest Robber Baronial temples of Modernism. All these years I, like so many others, had stood in front of a thousand, two thousand, God-knows-how-many thousand Pollocks, de Koonings, Newmans, Nolands, Rothkos, Rauschenbergs, Judds, Johnses, Olitskis, Louises, Stills, Franz Klines, Frankenthalers, Kellys, and Frank Stellas, now squinting, now popping the eye sockets open, now drawing back, now moving closer—waiting, waiting, forever waiting for ... *it* ... for *it* to come into focus, namely, the visual reward (for so much effort) which must be there, which everyone (*tout le monde*) knew to be there—waiting for something to radiate directly from the paintings on these invariably pure white walls, in this room, in this moment, into my own optic chiasma. All these years, in short, I had assumed that in art, if nowhere else, seeing is believing. Well—how very shortsighted! Now, at last, on April 28, 1974, I could see. I had gotten it backward all along. Not "seeing is believing," you ninny, but "believing is seeing," for *Modern Art has become completely literary: the paintings and other works exist only to illustrate the text.*

Like most sudden revelations, this one left me dizzy. How could such a thing be? How could Modern Art be *literary*? As every art-history student is told, the Modern movement began about 1900 with a complete rejection of the *literary* nature of academic art, meaning the sort of realistic art which originated in the Renaissance and which the various national academies still held up as the last word.

Literary became a code word for all that seemed hopelessly retrograde about realistic art. It probably referred originally to the way nineteenth-century painters liked to paint scenes straight from literature, such as Sir John Everett Millais's rendition of Hamlet's intended, *Ophelia,* floating dead (on her back) with a bouquet of wildflowers in her death grip. In time, *literary* came to refer to realistic painting in general. The idea was that half the power of a realistic painting comes not from the artist but from the sentiments the viewer hauls along to it, like so much mental baggage. According to this theory, the museum-going public's love of, say, Jean François Millet's *The Sower* has little to do with Millet's talent and everything to do with people's sentimental notions about The Sturdy Yeoman. They make up a little story about him.

What was the opposite of literary painting? Why, *l'art pour l'art,* form for the sake of form, color for the sake of color. In Europe before 1914, artists invented Modern styles with fanatic energy—Fauvism, Futurism, Cubism, Expressionism, Orphism, Supermatism, Vorticism—but everybody shared the same premise: henceforth, one doesn't paint "*about* anything, my dear aunt," to borrow a line from a famous *Punch* cartoon. One just *paints.* Art should no longer be a mirror held up to man or nature. A painting should compel the viewer to see it for what it is: a certain arrangement of colors and forms on a canvas.

Artists pitched in to help make theory. They loved it,

in fact. Georges Braque, the painter for whose work the word *Cubism* was coined, was a great formulator of precepts:

"The painter thinks in forms and colors. The aim is

Museum of Fine Arts, Bern, the Hermann and Margrit Rupf Collection

Georges Braque, *Houses at l'Estaque* (1908).

But not really houses, said Braque; rather, a certain arrangement of colors and forms on a canvas. ("Little cubes," said Matisse to the critic Louis Vauxcelles, who called Braque's new style "Cubism," thinking it a prize put-down.) The *Theory* starts here not to *reconstitute* an anecdotal fact but to *constitute* a pictorial fact."

Today this notion, this protest—which it was when Braque said it—has become a piece of orthodoxy. Artists repeat it endlessly, with conviction. As the Minimal Art movement came into its own in 1966, Frank Stella was saying it again:

"My painting is based on the fact that only what can be seen there *is* there. It really is an object . . . What you see is what you see."

Such emphasis, such certainty! What a head of steam—what patriotism an idea can build up in three-quarters of a century! In any event, so began Modern Art and so began the modern art of Art Theory. Braque, like Frank Stella, loved theory; but for Braque, who was a Montmartre boho* of the primitive sort, art came first. You can be sure the poor fellow never dreamed that during his own lifetime that order would be reversed.

* Twentieth-century American slang for *bohemian;* obverse of *hobo.*

Hot off the Carey airport bus, looking for lofts

The apache dance

ALL THE MAJOR MODERN MOVEMENTS EXCEPT FOR
de Stijl, Dada, Constructivism, and Surrealism began before the First World War, and yet they all
seem to come out of the 1920s. Why? Because it was in
the 1920s that Modern Art achieved social chic in Paris,
London, Berlin, and New York. Smart people talked
about it, wrote about it, enthused over it, and borrowed
from it. Borrowed from it, as I say; Modern Art
achieved the ultimate social acceptance: interior decorators did knockoffs of it in Belgravia and the sixteenth
arrondissement.

Things like knock-off specialists, money, publicity,
the smart set, and Le Chic shouldn't count in the history of art, as we all know—but, thanks to the artists
themselves, they do. Art and fashion are a two-backed

beast today; the artists can yell at fashion, but they can't move out ahead. That has come about as follows:

By 1900 the artist's arena—the place where he seeks honor, glory, ease, Success—had shifted twice. In seventeenth-century Europe the artist was literally, and also psychologically, the house guest of the nobility and the royal court (except in Holland); fine art and court art were one and the same. In the eighteenth century the scene shifted to the *salons,* in the homes of the wealthy bourgeoisie as well as those of aristocrats, where Culture-minded members of the upper classes held regular meetings with selected artists and writers. The artist was still the Gentleman, not yet the Genius. After the French Revolution, artists began to leave the *salons* and join *cénacles,* which were fraternities of like-minded souls huddled at some place like the Café Guerbois rather than a town house; around some romantic figure, an artist rather than a socialite, someone like Victor Hugo, Charles Nodier, Théophile Gautier, or, later, Edouard Manet. What held the *cénacles* together was that merry battle spirit we have all come to know and love: *épatez la bourgeoisie,* shock the middle class. With Gautier's *cénacle* especially . . . with Gautier's own red vests, black scarves, crazy hats, outrageous pronouncements, huge thirsts, and ravenous groin . . . the modern picture of The Artist began to form: the poor but free spirit, plebeian but aspiring only to be classless, to cut himself forever free from the bonds of the greedy and hypocritical bourgeoisie, to be whatever the fat burghers feared most, to cross the line wherever they drew it, to look at the world in a way

they couldn't see, to be high, live low, stay young forever—in short, to be the bohemian.

By 1900 and the era of Picasso, Braque & Co., the
modern game of Success in Art was pretty well set. As
a painter or sculptor the artist would do work that baf-
fled or subverted the cozy bourgeois vision of reality. As
an individual—well, that was a bit more complex. As a
bohemian, the artist had now left the *salons* of the upper classes—but he had not left their world. For getting
away from the bourgeoisie there's nothing like packing
up your paints and easel and heading for Tahiti, or even
Brittany, which was Gauguin's first stop. But who else
even got as far as Brittany? Nobody. The rest got no
farther than the heights of Montmartre and Montpar-
nasse, which are what?—perhaps two miles from the
Champs Elysées. Likewise in the United States: believe
me, you can get all the tubes of Winsor & Newton paint
you want in Cincinnati, but the artists keep migrating
to New York all the same . . . You can see them six days
a week . . . hot off the Carey airport bus, lined up in
front of the real-estate office on Broome Street in their
identical blue jeans, gum boots, and quilted Long
March jackets . . . looking, of course, for the inevitable
Loft . . .

No, somehow the artist wanted to remain within
walking distance . . . He took up quarters just around
the corner from . . . *le monde,* the social sphere described so well by Balzac, the milieu of those who find
it important to be *in fashion,* the orbit of those aristocrats, wealthy bourgeois, publishers, writers, journalists, impresarios, performers, who wish to be "where

Copyright Ronald Searle, 1961

Ronald Searle, *La Vie de Bohème*

things happen," the glamorous but small world of that creation of the nineteenth-century metropolis, *tout le monde,* Everybody, as in "Everybody says" . . . the smart set, in a phrase . . . "smart," with its overtones of cultivation as well as cynicism.

The ambitious artist, the artist who wanted Success, now had to do a bit of psychological double-tracking. Consciously he had to dedicate himself to the antibourgeois values of the *cénacles* of whatever sort, to bohemia, to the Bloomsbury life, the Left Bank life, the Lower Broadway Loft life, to the sacred squalor of it all, to the grim silhouette of the black Reo rig Lower Manhattan truck-route internal-combustion granules that were already standing an eighth of an inch thick on the poisoned roach carcasses atop the electric hotplate burner by the time you got up for breakfast . . . Not only that, he had to dedicate himself to the quirky god Avant-Garde. He had to keep one devout eye peeled for the new edge on the blade of the wedge of the head on the latest pick thrust of the newest exploratory probe of this fall's avant-garde Breakthrough of the Century . . . all this in order to make it, to be noticed, to be counted, within the community of artists themselves. What is more, he had to be *sincere* about it. At the same time he had to keep his other eye cocked to see if anyone in *le monde* was watching. *Have they noticed me yet?* Have they even noticed *the new style* (that me and my friends are working in)? Don't they even *know* about Tensionism (or Slice Art or Niho or Innerism or Dimensional Creamo or whatever)? (Hello, out there!) . . . because as every artist knew in his heart of hearts, no matter how many times he tried to close his eyes and pretend otherwise *(History! History!—where is thy salve?),* Success was *real* only when it was success within *le monde.*

He could close his eyes and try to believe that all that mattered was that *he* knew his work was great . . . and that other artists respected it . . . and that History would surely record his achievements . . . but deep down he knew he was lying to himself. *I want to be a Name, goddamn it!*—at least that, a name, a name on the lips of the museum curators, gallery owners, collectors, patrons, board members, committee members, Culture hostesses, and their attendant intellectuals and journalists and their *Time* and *Newsweek*—all right!—even that!—*Time* and *Newsweek*—Oh yes! (ask the shades of Jackson Pollock and Mark Rothko!)—even the god-damned journalists!

DURING THE 1960S THIS ENTIRE PROCESS BY WHICH *LE monde,* the culturati, scout bohemia and tap the young artist for Success was acted out in the most graphic way. Early each spring, two emissaries from the Museum of Modern Art, Alfred Barr and Dorothy Miller, would head downtown from the Museum on West Fifty-third Street, down to Saint Marks Place, Little Italy, Broome Street and environs, and tour the loft studios of known artists and unknowns alike, looking at everything, talking to one and all, trying to get a line on what was new and significant in order to put together a show in the fall . . . and, well, I mean, my God—from the moment the two of them stepped out on Fifty-third Street to grab a cab, some sort of boho radar began to record their sortie . . . *They're coming!* . . . And rolling across Lower Manhattan, like the Cosmic Pulse of the theosophists, would be a unitary heartbeat:

Pick me pick me pick me pick me pick me pick me pick me . . . O damnable Uptown!

By all means, deny it if asked!—what one knows, in one's cheating heart, and what one says are two different things!

So it was that the art mating ritual developed early in the century—in Paris, in Rome, in London, Berlin, Munich, Vienna, and, not too long afterward, in

New York. As we've just seen, the ritual has two phases:

1. The Boho Dance, in which the artist shows his stuff within the circles, coteries, movements, *isms,* of the home neighborhood, bohemia itself, as if he doesn't care about anything else; as if, in fact, he has a knife in his teeth against the fashionable world uptown.
2. The Consummation, in which culturati from that very same world, *le monde,* scout the various new movements and new artists of bohemia, select those who seem the most exciting, original, important, by whatever standards—and shower them with all the rewards of celebrity.

By the First World War the process was already like what in the Paris clip joints of the day was known as an apache dance. The artist was like the female in the act, stamping her feet, yelling defiance one moment, feigning indifference the next, resisting the advances of her pursuer with absolute contempt . . . more thrashing about . . . more rake-a-cheek fury . . . more yelling and carrying on . . . until finally with one last mighty and marvelously ambiguous shriek—*pain! ecstasy!*—she submits . . . Paff paff paff paff paff . . . How you do it, my boy! . . . and the house lights rise and Everyone, *tout le monde,* applauds . . .

The artist's payoff in this ritual is obvious enough. He stands to gain precisely what Freud says are the goals of the artist: fame, money, and beautiful lovers.

But what about *le monde,* the culturati, the social members of the act? What's in it for them? Part of their reward is the ancient and semi-sacred status of Benefactor of the Arts. The arts have always been a doorway into Society, and in the largest cities today the arts—the museum boards, arts councils, fund drives, openings, parties, committee meetings—have completely replaced the churches in this respect. But there is more!

Today there is a peculiarly modern reward that the

Gustave Doré. The Boho Dance

avant-garde artist can give his benefactor: namely, the feeling that he, like his mate the artist, is separate from and aloof from the bourgeoisie, the middle classes ... the feeling that he may be *from* the middle class but he is no longer *in* it ... the feeling that he is a fellow soldier, or at least an aide-de-camp or an honorary cong guerrilla in the vanguard march through the land of the philistines. This is a peculiarly modern need and a peculiarly modern kind of salvation (from the sin of Too Much Money) and something quite common among the well-to-do all over the West, in Rome and Milan as well as New York. That is why collecting contemporary art, the leading edge, the latest thing, warm and wet from the Loft, appeals specifically to those who feel most uneasy about their own commercial wealth ... See? I'm not like *them*—those Jaycees, those United Fund chairmen, those Young Presidents, those mindless New York A.C. *goyisheh* hog-jowled, stripe-tied goddamn-good-to-see-you-you-old-bastard-you oyster-bar trenchermen ... Avant-garde art, more than any other, takes the Mammon and the Moloch out of money, puts Levi's, turtlenecks, muttonchops, and other mantles and laurels of bohemian grace upon it.

That is why collectors today not only seek out the company of, but also want to hang out amidst, lollygag around with, and enter into the milieu of ... the artists they patronize. They *want* to climb those vertiginous loft building stairs on Howard Street that go up five flights without a single turn or bend—*straight up!* like something out of a casebook dream—to wind up with their hearts ricocheting around in their rib cages with tachycardia from the exertion mainly but also from the anticipation that just beyond this door at the top . . . in this loft . . . lie *the real goods* . . . paintings, sculptures that are indisputably part of the new movement, the new *école,* the new wave . . . something unshrinkable, chipsy, pure cong, bourgeois-proof.

The public is not invited
(and never has been)

NOW WE CÁN BEGIN TO UNDERSTAND HOW IT HAP-
pened that the Modernists, Braque & Bros., completed almost all their stylistic innovations before
the First World War, and yet Modern Art *seems* to belong to the postwar period. It is simply because the
Boho Dance took place before the war and the Consummation took place afterward. This is not what is so
often described as the lag between "the artist's discover-
ies" and "public acceptance." Public? The public plays
no part in the process whatsoever. The public is not invited (it gets a printed announcement later).

Le monde, the culturati, are no more a part of "the
public," the mob, the middle classes, than the artists are.
If it were possible to make one of those marvelous so-
ciometric diagrams that sociologists tried to perfect in

I'm still a virgin. (Where's the champagne?)

the 1950s, in which they tried to trace on a map the daily routes of key people in a community—a blue line for Community Leader A here and a red one for Leader B and a green one for Leader C and a broken sienna one for Bureaucrat Y, and so on—and the lines started moving around and intersecting here and there like a hallucinated Sony solid-state panel—if it were possible to make such a diagram of the art world, we would see that it is made up of (in addition to the artists) about 750 culturati in Rome, 500 in Milan, 1,750 in Paris, 1,250 in London, 2,000 in Berlin, Munich, and Düsseldorf, 3,000 in New York, and perhaps 1,000 scattered about the rest of the known world. That is the art world, approximately 10,000 souls—a mere hamlet!—restricted to *les beaux mondes* of eight cities.

The notion that the public accepts or rejects anything in Modern Art, the notion that the public scorns, ignores, fails to comprehend, allows to wither, crushes the spirit of, or commits any other crime against Art or any individual artist is merely a romantic fiction, a bittersweet Trilby sentiment. The game is completed and the trophies distributed long before the public knows what has happened. The public that buys books in hardcover and paperback by the millions, the public that buys records by the billions and fills stadiums for concerts, the public that spends $100 million on a single movie—this public affects taste, theory, and artistic outlook in literature, music, and drama, even though courtly elites hang on somewhat desperately in each field. The same has never been true in art. The public whose glorious numbers are recorded in the annual reports of the museums, all those students and bus tours and moms and

The Bettmann Archive

Pablo Picasso

dads and random intellectuals . . . are merely tourists, autograph seekers, gawkers, parade watchers, so far as the game of Success in Art is concerned. The public is presented with a *fait accompli* and the aforementioned printed announcement, usually in the form of a story or a spread of color pictures in the back pages of *Time*. An announcement, as I say. Not even the most powerful organs of the press, including *Time, Newsweek,* and *The New York Times,* can discover a new artist or certify his worth and make it stick. They can only bring you the news, tell you which artists the *beau* hamlet, Cultureburg, has discovered and certified. They can only bring you the scores.

We can now also begin to see that Modern Art enjoyed all the glories of the Consummation stage after

the First World War not because it was "finally understood" or "finally appreciated" but rather because a few
fashionable people discovered *their own uses* for it. It
was after the First World War that *modern* and *modernistic* came into the language as exciting adjectives
(somewhat like *now,* as in the *Now Generation,* during
the 1960s). By 1920, in *le monde,* to be fashionable was
to be *modern,* and Modern Art and the new spirit of the
avant-garde were perfectly suited for that vogue.

Picasso is a case in point. Picasso did not begin to become *Picasso,* in the art world or in the press, until he
was pushing forty and painted the scenery for Diaghilev's Russian ballet in London in 1918. Diaghilev &
Co. were a tremendous *succès de scandale* in fashionable
London. The wild dervishing of Nijinsky, the lurid
costumes—it was all too deliciously *modern* for words.
The Modernistic settings by Picasso, André Derain,
and (later on) Matisse, were all part of the excitement,
and *le monde* loved it. "Art," in Osbert Lancaster's
phrase, "came once more to roost among the
duchesses."

Picasso, who had once lived in the legendary unlit attic and painted at night with a brush in one hand and a
candlestick in the other—Picasso now stayed at the
Savoy, had lots of clothes made on Bond Street and
nearby, including a set of tails, went to all the best parties (and parties were never better), was set up with
highly publicized shows of his paintings, and became a
social lion—which he remained, Tales of the Aging
Recluse notwithstanding, until he was in his seventies.

Back in Paris, the new Picasso turned up at the theater with his kid gloves, canes, tall hats, capes, and din-

ner clothes, and the linings gave you a little silk flash
every time he wheeled about in the lobby to chat with
one of his hellish new friends ... Our old pal Braque
shook his head sadly ... At least Derain had had the
decency to confine himself to a blue serge suit when *he*
was being lionized in London, and he had stuck to the
company of local bohos in his off hours ... But Picasso—Braque was like that incorruptible member of
the Cénacle of the rue des Quatre Vents, Daniel
D'Arthez, watching the decay of Lucien Chardon in
Balzac's *Lost Illusions.* With a sigh Braque waited for
his old comrade Pablo's imminent collapse as a painter
and a human being ... But the damnedest thing happened instead! Picasso just kept ascending, to El Do-
rado, to tremendous wealth but to much more than
that, to the sainted status of *Picasso,* to the point where
by 1950 he was known at every level of opinion, from
Art News to the *Daily News,* as *the* painter of the twentieth century. As for Derain and his blue serge suit and
Braque and his scruples—the two old boys, both very
nearly the same age as Picasso, i.e., about seventy, were
remembered in 1950 chiefly as part of the pit crew during Picasso's monumental victory.*

Not to beg the question of differences in talent—but
here we have the classic demonstration of the artist who
knows how to double-track his way from the Boho
Dance to the Consummation as opposed to the artist
who gets stuck forever in the Boho Dance. This is an
ever-present hazard of the art mating ritual. Truly suc-

---

* History, kind history, has improved Braque's status considerably since his death
in 1963.

cessful double-tracking requires the artist to be a sincere and committed performer in *both roles.* Many artists become so dedicated to bohemian values, internalize their antibourgeois feelings so profoundly, that they are unable to cut loose, let go, with that cathartic shriek—*pain! ectasy!* paff paff paff paff paff paff—and submit gracefully to good fortune; the sort of artist, and his name is Legion, who always comes to the black-tie openings at the Museum of Modern Art wearing a dinner jacket and paint-spattered Levi's .... *I'm still a virgin!* (Where's the champagne?)

chapter III

Le Tout New York on
a Cubist horse

SO MODERN ART ENJOYED A TREMENDOUS SOCIAL boom in Europe in the 1920s. And what about the United States? A painter, Marsden Hartley, wrote in 1921 that "art in America is like a patent medicine or a vacuum cleaner. It can hope for no success until ninety million people know what it is." Bitter stuff! In fact, however, he couldn't have gotten it more precisely wrong. Modern Art was a success in the United States in no time—as soon as a very few people knew what it was, the 400, as it were, as opposed to the 90 million.

These were New Yorkers of wealth and fashion, such as the Rockefellers and Goodyears, who saw their counterparts in London enjoying the chic and excitement of Picasso, Derain, Matisse, and the rest of *Le Moderne* and who wanted to import it for themselves.

"Hitch your wagon to a star." —Ralph Waldo Emerson

This they did. Modern Art arrived in the United States in the 1920s not like a rebel commando force but like Standard Oil. By 1929 it had been established, *institutionalized,* in the most overwhelming way: in the form of the Museum of Modern Art. This cathedral of Culture was not exactly the brain child of visionary bohemians. It was founded in John D. Rockefeller, Jr.'s living room, to be exact, with Goodyears, Blisses, and Crowninshields in attendance.

Against such a vogue in *le monde,* conservative critics in New York were helpless. Their very base no longer existed. The doyen of the breed, Royal Cortissoz, made a mighty effort, however. Writing in 1923, at the time of a national debate over immigration (which led to the Immigration Act of 1924), he compared the alien invasion of European modernism to the subversive alien hordes coming in by boat. "Ellis Island art," he called it, no doubt figuring he had come up with a devastating label. Well!—as one can imagine!—how everybody sniggered at poor Mr. Cortissoz over that!

By the mid-1930s, Modern Art was already so chic that corporations held it aloft like a flag to show that they were both up-to-date and enlightened, a force in Culture as well as commerce. The Dole Pineapple Company sent Georgia O'Keeffe and Isamu Noguchi to Hawaii to record their impressions, and the Container Corporation of America was commissioning abstract work by Fernand Léger, Henry Moore, and others. This led to the Container Corporation's long-running advertising campaign, the Great Ideas of Western Man series, in which it would run a Great Idea by a noted savant at the top of the page, one of them being "'Hitch your wagon to a star'—Ralph Waldo Emerson." Underneath would be a picture of a Cubist horse strangling on a banana.

Naturally the chic of *Le Moderne* put a heavy burden on theory. Each new movement, each new *ism* in Modern Art was a declaration by the artists that they had a new way of seeing which the rest of the world (read: the bourgeoisie) couldn't comprehend. "We understand!" said the culturati, thereby separating themselves also from the herd. But what inna namea Christ *were* the artists seeing? This was where theory came in. A hundred years before, Art Theory had merely been something that enriched one's conversation in matters of Culture. Now it was an absolute necessity. It was no longer background music. It was an essential hormone in the mating ritual. *All we ask for is a few lines of explanation!* You say Meret Oppenheim's *Fur-Covered Cup, Saucer and Spoon* (the *pièce de résistance* of the Museum of Modern Art's Surrealism show in December 1936) is an example of the Surrealist principle of displacement? You say the texture of one material—fur—has been imposed upon the forms of others—china and tableware—in order to split the oral, the tactile, and the visual into three critically injured but for the first time fiercely independent parties in the subconscious? Fine. To get the word was to understand. The Dadaists professed to be furious over this obscene embrace by the very people they had been attacking. "Any work of art that can be understood is the product of a journalist," said Tristan Tzara's Dada manifesto. "So what?" came the reply. ("You dismal little Rumanian.") Even an explanation of why one couldn't accept something, including Dada, was explanation enough to accept it.

Yet Theory did not come fully into its own, triumphant, transcendent, more important than painting and sculpture themselves, until after the Second World War. Theory, this first-class coach on the Freight Train of History (to use a phrase from the period), was held back by a little matter that seldom finds its way into the art histories today, as if what the Freudians call "the amnesia of childhood" were at work. For more than ten years, from about 1930 to 1941, the artists themselves, in Europe and America, suspended the Modern movement . . . for the duration, as it were . . . They called it off! They suddenly returned to "literary" realism of the most obvious sort, a genre known as Social Realism.

Left politics did that for them. Left politicians said, in effect: You artists claim to be dedicated to an anti-bourgeois life. Well, the hour has now come to stop merely posing and to take action, to turn your art into a weapon. Translation: propaganda paintings. The influence of Left politics was so strong within the art world during the 1930s that Social Realism became not a style of the period but *the* style of the period. Even the most dedicated Modernists were intimidated. Years later Barnett Newman wrote that the "shouting dogmatists, Marxist, Leninist, Stalinist, and Trotskyite" created "an intellectual prison that locked one in tight." I detect considerable amnesia today on that point. All best forgotten! Artists whose names exist as little more than footnotes today—William Gropper, Ben Shahn, Jack Levine—were *giants* as long as the martial music of the mimeograph machines rolled on in a thousand Protest Committee rooms. For any prominent critic of the time to have written off Ben Shahn as a commercial illustrator, as Barbara Rose did recently, would have touched off a brawl. Today no one cares, for Social Realism evaporated with the political atmosphere that generated it. By 1946 the scene had cleared for the art of our day—an art more truly Literary than anything ever roared against in the wildest angers of the Fauvists and Cubists.

chapter

IV

Greenberg, Rosenberg & Flat

NONE OF THE ABSTRACT EXPRESSIONIST PAINTINGS
that remain from the palmy days of 1946 to 1960—
and precious few are still hanging except in museums and the guest bedrooms of Long Island
beachhouses, back there with the iron bedstead whose
joints don't gee, the Russel Wright water pitcher left
over from the set of dishes the newlyweds bought for
their first apartment after the war, and an Emerson radio with tubes and a shortwave band . . . none of the
paintings, as I say, not even Jackson Pollock's and
Willem de Kooning's, makes quite as perfect a memor-
ial to that brave and confident little epoch as the Theories. As for the paintings—*de gustibus non disputandum
est.* But the theories, I insist, were *beautiful.*

Theories? They were more than theories, they were

When Flat was God. Using the impastometer

mental constructs. No, more than that even ... veritable edifices behind the eyeballs they were ... castles in the cortex ... mezuzahs on the pyramids of Betz ... crystalline ... comparable in their bizarre refinements to medieval Scholasticism.

We can understand the spellbinding effect these theories had, however, only by keeping in mind what we have noted so far: (1) the art world is a small town; (2) part of the small town, *le monde,* always looks to the other, bohemia, for *the new wave* and is primed to believe in it; (3) bohemia is made up of *cénacles,* schools, coteries, circles, cliques. Consequently, should one *cénacle* come to dominate bohemia, its views might very well dominate the entire small town (a.k.a. "the art world"), all the way from the Chambers Street station to Eighty-ninth and Fifth.

And that is precisely what happened in New York after the Second World War in the era of Abstract Expressionism, when New York replaced Paris (as one was so often reminded) as the county seat of Modernism.

During the Dark Ages—i.e., the 1930s interlude of Social Realism—small *cénacles* of Modernists kept the faith alive down in bohemia, down below Fourteenth Street. They were like a real underground, for a change—in hiding this time not from that rather metaphysical menace, the bourgeoisie, but from their own comrade bohemian drillmasters, the aforementioned "shouting dogmatists" of the Left. Even Franz Kline, the abstract painter's abstract painter, was dutifully cranking out paintings of unemployed Negroes, crippled war veterans, and the ubiquitous workers with the open blue work shirts and necks wider than their heads. But there were those who kept Modernism alive . . .

The most influential *cénacle* centered upon Hans Hofmann, a German painter in his mid-fifties who simply ignored the drillmasters and ran his art school in Greenwich Village as a philosophical outpost for *l'art pour l'art* and abstract painting. Another *cénacle* met in the studio of a sculptor, Ibram Lassaw; this one included Ad Reinhardt and Josef Albers and eventually grew into an organization called American Abstract Artists. The Triple A seemed to be animated mainly by anger at *le monde,* and the Whitney Museum and the Museum of Modern Art particularly, for patronizing European abstract work (and, if one need edit, not theirs). Another circle of friends, Adolph Gottlieb, Mark Rothko, and Milton Avery among them, was known as "the Ten." Another gathered about John Graham and included de Kooning, Arshile Gorky, Stuart Davis, and David Smith. Still another included Roberto Matta, William Baziotes, and Jackson Pollock, who was married to a member of the Hofmann *cénacle,* Lee Krasner, bringing us full circle.

ALL THESE CIRCLES AND COTERIES CAME TOGETHER after the war as the *cénacle des cénacles,* the New York School, or Tenth Street School, creators of Abstract Expressionism. Most of these people had slogged their way through the Depression with great difficulty, and their mood tended toward bohemianism of the High Seriousness vein.

Two of their main meeting places, the Subjects of the Artist School and The Club, were on East Eighth Street, and the other, the Cedar Tavern, was on University Place. But the galleries that showed their work, such as the Area and the Hilda Carmel, were on Tenth Street, and that was the name that caught on. Within *le monde,* "going down to Tenth Street" was like the Saturday pilgrimage "down to Soho" today. In any event,

Fred W. McDarrah

The Cedar Tavern, scene of the *cénacle des cénacles* and one of Cultureburg's most prestigious boho cafés of all time, comparable to the Five Spot, the White Horse, and Max's Kansas City. "Hi, Marko!"

this *cénacle* was soon so big and so influential that the regular Friday night meetings at The Club became like town meetings for the entire New York art scene, attracting dealers, collectors, uptown curators like Alfred Barr, critics, and just about any other culturati who could wangle their way in.

The great theorists to come out of this *cénacle des cénacles* were Clement Greenberg and Harold Rosenberg. Both had been involved in the Lower Manhattan Left literary politics of the 1930s, then became more and more purely theorists, critics, aestheticians in the 1940s. More to the point, both had been friends of various abstract artists even during the Freeze. Greenberg had been a regular in the Hofmann *cénacle*—and it was essentially Hofmann's ideas and Hofmann's emphasis on purity *purity* **purity** that were about to sweep Cultureburg, via Greenberg. One secret of Greenberg's and Rosenberg's astounding success, then, was that they were not like uptown critics—they were not *mere* critics: they spoke as the voice of bohemia . . . and naturally *le monde* listened.

To describe this, the well-placed platform they spoke from, is not to downgrade the two men's peculiar genius. Greenberg, in particular, radiated a sense of absolute *authority*. He was not a very prepossessing individual at first glance. He spoke in fits and starts one minute and drawls the next. But somehow one couldn't help but pay attention. Likewise his prose style: he would veer from the most skull-crushing Göttingen Scholar tautologies, "essences" and "purities" and "opticalities" and "formal factors" and "logics of readjustment" and God knows what else . . . to cries of despair and outrage such as would have embarrassed Shelley. In a famous essay in *Horizon* in 1947 he said the entire future of art in America was in the hands of fifty brave but anonymous and beleagured artists "south of 34th Street" who were about to be wiped out at any moment. By whom—by what? Why, by the "dull horror" of American life. "Their isolation is inconceivably crushing, unbroken, damning," said Greenberg. "That anyone can produce art on a respectable level in this situation is highly improbable. What can fifty do against a hundred and forty million?"

Fifty against 140 million! Beautiful; he had out-Hartleyed Marsden Hartley; Hartley's scouting report on the enemy back in 1921 listed only 90 million. It was all sheer rhetoric, of course, the antibourgeois sing-along of bohemia, standard since the 1840s, as natural as breathing by now and quite marvelously devoid of any rational content—and yet Greenberg pulled it off with—well, not just with authority but with *moral* authority. When Greenberg spoke, it was as if not merely the future of Art were at stake but the very quality, the very *possibility,* of civilization in America. His fury seemed to come out of an implacable insistence on *purity.* He saw Modernism as heading toward a certain inevitable conclusion, through its own internal logic, just as Marxists saw Western society as heading irrevocably toward the dictatorship of the proletariat and an ensuing nirvana. In Greenberg's eyes, the Freight Train of Art History had a specific destination. He called for "self-criticism" and "self-definition"—"self-definition with a vengeance," he said. It was time to clear the tracks at last of all the remaining rubble of the pre-

Modern way of painting. And just what was this destination? On this point Greenberg couldn't have been clearer: *Flatness.*

The general theory went as follows: as the Cubists and other early Modernists had correctly realized, a painting was not a window through which one could peer into the distance. The three-dimensional effects were sheer illusion (et ergo ersatz). A painting was a flat surface with paint on it. Earlier abstract artists had understood the importance of flatness in the simple sense of painting in two dimensions, but they hadn't known how to go beyond that. They still used paint in such a way that it divided neatly into lines, forms, contours, and colors, just as it had in pre-Modern days. What was needed was *purity*—a style in which lines, forms, contours, colors all became unified on the flat surface.

This business of flatness became quite an issue; an

© *1973 Arnold Newman*

Clement Greenberg

obsession, one might say. The question of what an artist could or could not do without violating the principle of Flatness—"the integrity of the picture plane," as it became known—inspired such subtle distinctions, such exquisitely miniaturized hypotheses, such stereotactic microelectrode needle-implant hostilities, such brilliant if ever-decreasing tighter-turning spirals of logic . . . that it compares admirably with the most famous of all questions that remain from the debates of the Scholastics: "How many angels can dance on the head of a pin?"

MOST OF THE THEORY UP TO 1950 WAS GREENBERGIAN in origin. Enter Rosenberg. Rosenberg came up with a higher synthesis, a theory that combined Greenberg's formal purity with something that had been lacking in abstract art from the early Synthetic Cubist days and ever since: namely, the emotional wallop of the old realistic pre-Modern pictures. This was a question that

Harold Rosenberg

had troubled Picasso throughout the 1930s. Any return to realism was out, of course, but Rosenberg had a solution: "Action Painting," which became the single most famous phrase of the period (a fact that did not please Greenberg).

"At a certain moment the canvas began to appear to one American painter after another as an arena in which to act," said Rosenberg. "What was to go on the canvas was not a picture but an event." The vision that Rosenberg inspired caught the public imagination for a time (the actual *public*!) as well as that of more painters, professional and amateur, than one is likely to want to recall. It was of Action Painter ... a Promethean artist gorged with emotion and overloaded with paint, hurling himself and his brushes at the canvas as if in hand-to-hand combat with Fate. *There!* ... *there!* ... *there* in those furious swipes of the brush on canvas, in those splatters of unchained id, one could see the artist's emotion itself—still alive!—in the finished product. (And see? All the picture-plane integrity a reasonable man could ask for, and lines that are forms and forms that are colors and colors that are both.)

It is important to repeat that Greenberg and Rosenberg did not create their theories in a vacuum or simply turn up with them one day like tablets brought down from atop Green Mountain or Red Mountain (as B. H. Friedman once called the two men). As *tout le monde* understood, they were not only theories but ... hot news, straight from the studios, from the scene. Rosenberg's famous Action Painting piece in *Art News* did not mention a single new artist by name, but *tout le monde* knew that when he spoke of "one American painter after another" taking up the style, he was really talking about one American painter: his friend de Kooning . . . or perhaps de Kooning and his *cénacle*. Greenberg's main man, as Everybody knew, was his friend Pollock.

Greenberg didn't discover Pollock or even create his reputation, as was said so often later on. Damnable Uptown did that. *Pick me!* Peggy Guggenheim picked Pollock. He was a nameless down-and-out boho Cubist. She was the niece of Solomon (Guggenheim Museum) Guggenheim and the center of the most chic Uptown art circle in New York in the 1940s, a circle featuring famous Modern artists from Europe (including her husband, Max Ernst) who were fleeing the war, Uptown intellectuals such as Alfred Barr and James Johnson Sweeney of the Museum of Modern Art, and young boho protégés such as two members of Pollock's *cénacle,* Baziotes and Robert Motherwell. In a single year, 1943, Peggy Guggenheim met Pollock through Baziotes and Motherwell, gave him a monthly stipend, got him moving in the direction of Surrealist "automatic writing" (she loved Surrealism), set him up on Fifty-seventh Street—Uptown Street of Dreams!— with his first show—in the most chic Modernist salon in the history of New York, her own Art of This Century Gallery, with its marvelous Surrealist Room, where the pictures were mounted on baseball bats—got Sweeney to write the catalogue introduction, in prose that ranged from merely rosy to deep purple dreams— and Barr inducted one of the paintings, *The She Wolf,* into the Museum of Modern Art's Permanent Collection—and Motherwell wrote a rave for *Partisan Re-*

Hans Namuth

De Kooning in his studio in mid-Action:
the bull—or the matador—as you like it—pulls back
and takes a few snorts of reflection before the next
collision with Fate

view—and Greenberg wrote a super-rave for *The Nation* . . . and, well, Greenberg was rather late getting into the loop, if anything. The Consummation was complete and Pollock was a Success before the last painting was hung and the doors were opened and the first Manhattan was poured (remember Manhattans?) on opening night. To that extent Greenberg was just an ordinary reporter bringing you the latest news.

But Greenberg did something more than discover Pollock or establish him. He used Pollock's certified success to put over Flatness as *the* theory—the theoretical breakthrough of Einstein-scale authority—of the entire new wave of the Tenth Street *cénacle des cénacles*.

"Pollock's strength," he would say, "lies in the emphatic surfaces of his pictures, which it is his concern to maintain and intensify in all that thick, fuliginous flatness which began—but only began—to be the strong point of late Cubism." And all through bohemia the melody played . . . *That thick, fuliginous flatness got me in its spell* . . . "It is the tension inherent in the constructed, re-created flatness of the surface," Greenberg would say, "that produces the strength of his art" . . . *That constructed, re-created flatness that you weave so well* . . . "his concentration on surface texture and tactile qualities" . . . *Those famous paint-flings on that picture plane* . . .

AH, THE MUSIC WAS PLAYING! AND CLEMENT GREENberg was the composer! Other artists were picking up on his theories and Rosenberg's, sometimes by reading them in the journals—*Partisan Review, The Nation,*

Horizon—but more often in conversation. With The Club going down on Eighth Street the artists of bohemia were now meeting all the time, every day, and talking up a storm. They outtalked any ten canasta clubs from Oceanside and Cedarhurst.

Greenberg was no slouch at conversation himself, despite his jerky windups and his not very elegant deliveries. Somehow the rough edges went perfectly with the *moral conviction* that seemed to radiate from his eyeballs. A forty-one-year-old Washington, D.C., artist

Collection, The Museum of Modern Art, New York

Jackson Pollock's *The She Wolf* (1943), the painting
the Museum of Modern Art bought as its part in
Pollock's Consummation. The style is halfway between
Pollock's early Picasso-Cubist style and the completely
abstract "drip" style for which Pollock is best known.
That thick, fuliginous flatness got me in its spell . . .

named Morris Louis came to New York in 1953 to try
to get a line on what was going on in this new wave,
and he had some long talks with Greenberg, and the

Collection, The Museum of Modern Art, New York

Morris Louis, *Third Element*, 1962.

No painter ever took the Word more literally; with the possible exception of Frank Stella whole experience changed his life. He went back to Washington and began thinking. *Flatness,* the man had said . . . (You bet he had) . . . The spark flew, and Louis saw the future with great clarity. The very use of thick oil paint itself had been a crime against flatness, a violation of the integrity of the picture plane, all these years . . . But of course! Even in the hands of Picasso, ordinary paint was likely to build up as much as a millimeter or two *above* mean canvas level! And as for the new Picasso—i.e., Pollock—my God, get out a ruler!

So Louis used unprimed canvas and thinned out his paint until it *soaked right into* the canvas when he brushed it on. He could put a painting on the floor and lie on top of the canvas and cock his eye sideways like a robin and look along the surface of the canvas—and he had done it! Nothing existed above or below the picture plane, except for a few ultramicroscopic wisps of cotton fray, and what reasonable person could count that against him . . . No, everything now existed precisely *in* the picture plane and nowhere else. The paint was the picture plane, and the picture plane was the paint. Did I hear the word *flat?*—well, try to out-flat this, you young Gotham rascals! Thus was born an offshoot of Abstract Expressionism known as the Washington School. A man from Mars or Chester, Pa., incidentally, would have looked at a Morris Louis painting and seen rows of rather watery-looking stripes.

But the Washington School or the Tenth Street School was no place for creatures from out of state unless they'd had their coats pulled, unless they'd been briefed on the theories. In no time these theories of flatness, of abstractness, of pure form and pure color, of expressive brushwork ("action") seemed no longer mere theories but axioms, part of the given, as basic as the Four Humors had once seemed in any consideration of human health. Not to know about these things was not to have the Word.

The Word—but exactly. A curious change was taking place at the very core of the business of being a painter. Early Modernism had been a reaction to nineteenth-century realism, an abstraction of it, a diagram of it, to borrow John Berger's phrase, just as a blueprint is a diagram of a house. But this Abstract Expressionism of the Tenth Street School was a reaction to earlier Modernism itself, to Cubism chiefly. It was an abstraction of an abstraction, a blueprint of the blueprint, a diagram of the diagram—and a diagram of a diagram is metaphysics. Anyone who tries making a diagram of a diagram will see why. Metaphysics can be dazzling!—as dazzling as the Scholastics and their wing commands of Angels and Departed Souls. But somehow the ethereal little dears are inapprehensible without words. In short, the new order of things in the art world was: first you get the Word, and then you can see.

The artists themselves didn't seem to have the faintest notion of how primary Theory was becoming. I wonder if the theorists themselves did. All of them, artists and theorists, were talking as if their conscious aim was to create a totally immediate art, lucid, stripped of all the dreadful baggage of history, an art fully revealed, honest, as honest as the flat-out integral picture plane. "Aesthetics is for the artists as ornithology is for the birds," said Barnett Newman in a much-repeated *mot*. And yet Newman himself happened to be one of the most incessant theoreticians on Eighth Street, and his work showed it. He spent the last twenty-two years of his life studying the problems (if any) of dealing with big areas of color divided by stripes . . . on a flat picture plane. Nobody was immune to theory any longer. Pollock would say things like "Cézanne didn't create theories. They're after the fact." He was only whistling "Dixie." The fact was that theories—Greenberg's—about Pollock—were beginning to affect Pollock. Greenberg hadn't created Pollock's rep-

Hans Namuth

Barnett Newman

Hans Namuth

Jackson Pollock

utation, but he *was* its curator, custodian, brass polisher, and repairman, and he was terrific at it. With each new article Greenberg edged Pollock's status a little higher, from "among the strongest" American abstract artists ever to "the strongest painter of his generation" in America to "the most powerful painter in contemporary America" to a neck-and-neck competition with John Marin (John Marin!) for the title of "the greatest American painter of the twentieth century." To the few remaining dissidents, Uptown or Downtown, who still pulled long faces and said Pollock's work looked terribly "muddy" or "chaotic" or simply "ugly," Greenberg had a marvelous comeback: but of course!—"all profoundly original art looks ugly at first." Well . . . yes! *That's . . . right!* In an age of avant-gardism, when practically everybody in Cultureburg could remember some new *ism* which he "hadn't gotten" at first, this Greenberg dictum seemed to be a pivotal insight of Modernism, the golden *aperçu.* To collectors, curators, and even some dealers, new work that looked genuinely *ugly* . . . began to take on a strange new glow . . .

In any event, if Greenberg was right about Pollock's status in the world of art—and Pollock wasn't arguing—then he must also be right about the theories. So Pollock started pushing his work in the direction the theories went. Onward! Flatter! More fuliginous! More "over-all evenness"! But fewer gaping holes! (Greenberg thought Pollock sometimes left "gaping holes" in the otherwise "integrated plane.") Greenberg took to going by Pollock's studio and giving on-the-spot critiques.

Soon Pollock was having a generally hard time figuring out where the boundary was between Himself—old Jack—and his Reputation or whether there was any. Pollock was the classic case of the artist hopelessly stuck between the Boho Dance and the Consummation. Pollock had internalized the usual antibourgeois bohemian values in huge gulps during the days of the Depression, when he was a boho on the dole and doing odd jobs such as hand-painting neckties (during that short-lived men's fashion). The Consummation came so fast—in that one year, 1943—Pollock never could manage the double-tracking. He got forever stuck halfway. Here was the archetypical Pollock gesture: one night he arrives drunk at Peggy Guggenheim's house during a party for a lot of swell people. So he takes off his clothes in another room and comes walking into the living room stark naked and urinates in the fireplace. On the other hand, neither that night nor thereafter did he give up coming to Peggy Guggenheim's house, where all those swell people were. He would insist on going to the old Stork Club or to 21 without a necktie to prove he could get in anyway thanks to "my reputation"—and if he did, he would make sure he got drunk enough and rude enough to get thrown out. They had to accept him Uptown, but he couldn't stand liking it.

Despite his huge reputation, his work did not sell well, and he barely scraped by financially—which satisfied his boho soul on the one hand but also made him scream (stuck, as he was, in the doorway): *If I'm so terrific, why ain't I rich?* And this gets down to the problems that collectors were beginning to have with Abstract Expressionism and the abstract styles that followed, such as the Washington School. Most of early Modernism, and particularly Cubism, was only partly abstract. The creatures in Matisse's *Joie de Vivre,* which seemed so outrageously abstract in 1905, may not have been nice concupiscent little lamb chops such as were available in Max Klinger's *The Judgment of Paris,* but they were nude women all the same. For many collectors it was enough to know the general theory and the fact that here were nudes done in "the new [Fauvist, Cubist, Expressionist, Surrealist, or whatever] way." But with Abstract Expressionism and what came after it, they had to have . . . the Word. There were no two ways about it. There was no use whatsoever in looking at a picture without knowing about Flatness and associated theorems.

How manfully they tried! How they squinted and put their fingers under their eyelids in order to focus more sharply (as Greenberg was said to do) . . . how they tried to *internalize* the theories to the point where they could *feel* a tingle or two *at the very moment* they looked at an abstract painting . . . without first having to give the script a little run-through in their minds. And some succeeded. But *all tried*! I stress that in light of the terrible charges some of the Abstractionists and their theorists are making today against the collectors . . . calling them *philistines* and *nouveaux-riches, status strivers* who only *pretended* to like abstract art, even during the heyday of the 1950s. Which is to say: You were nothing but fat middle-class fakes all along! You never had a true antibourgeois bone in your bodies!

AH, INGRATITUDE, INGRATITUDE . . . *ARS LONGA MEMORIA brevis* . . . The truth was that the collectors wanted nothing more than to believe wholeheartedly, to march with the Abstract Expressionists as aides-de-cong through the land of the philistines. They *believed,* along with the artists, that Abstract Expressionism was *the final form,* that painting had at last gone extra-atmospheric, into outer space, into a universe of pure forms and pure colors. Even Cultureburg's intellectual fringe, the journalists of the popular press, reported the news in good faith, without a snigger. In 1949 *Life* magazine gave Pollock a three-page spread, two of them in color, headed: "JACKSON POLLOCK. Is he the greatest living painter in the United States?" The whole piece was clearly derived from the say-so of Greenberg, whom *Life* identified as "a formidably high-brow New York critic." *Life, Time, Newsweek* continued to follow Abstract Expressionism, in color, with the occasional 22-caliber punnery about "Jack the Dripper" (Pollock) who says little and "stands on his painting," but also with the clear message that this was what was important in contemporary art.

In fact, the press was so attentive that Harold Rosenberg, as well as Pollock, wondered why so little Abstract Expressionism was being bought. "Considering the degree to which it is publicized and feted," Rosenberg said, "vanguard painting is hardly bought at all." Here Rosenberg was merely betraying the art world's blindness toward its own strategies. He seemed to believe that there was an art public in the same sense that there was a reading public and that, consequently, there should be some sort of public demand for the latest art objects. He was doing the usual, in other words. First you do everything possible to make sure your world is antibourgeois, that it defies bourgeois tastes, that it mystifies the mob, the public, that it outdistances the insensible middle-class multitudes by light-years of subtlety and intellect—and then, having succeeded admirably, you ask with a sense of *See-what-I-mean?* outrage: look, they don't even buy our products! (Usually referred to as "quality art.") The art world had been successfully restricted to about 10,000 souls worldwide, the *beaux mondes* of a few metropolises. Of these, perhaps 2,000 were collectors, and probably no more than 300—worldwide—bought current work (this year's, last year's, the year-before's) with any regularity; of these, perhaps 90 lived in the United States.

There were brave and patriotic collectors who created a little flurry of activity on the Abstract Expressionist market in the late 1950s, but in general this type of painting was depreciating faster than a Pontiac Bonneville once it left the showroom. The resale market was a shambles. Without the museums to step in here and there, to buy in the name of history, Abstract Expressionism was becoming a real beached whale commercially. The deep-down mutter-to-myself truth was that the collectors, despite their fervent desire to be virtuous, had never been able to build up any gusto for Abstract Expressionism. Somehow that six-flight walk up the spiral staircase of Theory took the wind out of you.

I once heard Robert Scull say, "Abstract Expressionism was a little club down on Tenth Street. There were never more than 100 people in on it." Scull was a collector from a later, enemy camp, Pop Art, and he may have set the figure too low, but I suspect that he was, at the core, correct. As was the case with Swedenborgianism and Rosicrucianism, Abstract Expressionism's makers and theorists and its truly committed audience seem to have been one and the same. Who else was there, really, but the old *cénacles* down on Eighth Street . . . unless you also count the interior decorators who did *truly love* to use Abstract Expressionist paintings with those large flat areas (O integral planes!) of bright color to set off the stark white apartments that were so fashionable at the time.

But to say that Abstract Expressionism was a baby that only its parents could love is not to downgrade its theorists in the slightest. Quite the opposite. For a good fifteen years, with nothing going for them except brain power and stupendous rectitude and the peculiar makeup of the art world, they projected this style, this unloved brat of theirs, until it filled up the screen of art history.

Hello, Steinberg
(Goodbye, Greenberg)
(You, too, Rosenberg)
(Joy returns to Cultureburg)

WE MAY STATE IT AS A PRINCIPLE AT THIS POINT that collectors of contemporary art do not want to buy highly abstract art unless it's the only game in town. They will always prefer realistic art instead—as long as someone in authority assures them that it is (a) new, and (b) not realistic. To understand this contradiction is to understand what happened next: Pop Art.

One day—in 1963, it must have been—I ran into a magazine editor, a culturatus of sorts, and I happened to bring up the subject of Abstract Expressionism, whereupon he told me with a tone that indicated I must be the only person in town who hadn't gotten the inside news: "Listen, Abstract Expressionism is dead. It's been finished off by a professor at Hunter College, a guy named Leo Steinberg."

Andy Warhol. Nothing is more bourgeois than to be
afraid to look bourgeois

I don't know that Steinberg finished off Abstract Expressionism. It only needed a little push. But Steinberg was certainly one of the authorities who made it okay to like Pop Art.

The Pop Art era is usually dated from the first one-man show of Jasper Johns at the Leo Castelli Gallery, January 20 to February 8, 1958, with paintings of American flags, letters of the alphabet, rows of numbers, and archery targets. Johns and his friend Robert Rauschenberg were the major figures in a *cénacle* of younger artists who in the 1950s began to react against the by-now sainted Abstract Expressionists. Young artists had started pouring into Lower Manhattan and heading, naturally, for legendary spots like the Cedar Tavern. They liked to pop into the Cedar with their toggle coats and corduroys and other proper boho gear on, like

Mark Feldstein

Leo Steinberg

Hans Namuth   *Hans Namuth*

Jasper Johns and Robert Rauschenberg, the two early
imps of Pop Art

young recruits ready for the battle against the blind
public, and they'd say, "Hi, Bill!" (de Kooning), "Hi,
Franz!" (Kline), "Whaddaya say, Marko!" (Rothko).
But the old boys didn't exactly feel like being buddies
and sharing the glow with these hideously chummy
young nobodies. All right . . . So Johns and Rauschenberg started zapping the old bastards in their weakest
spot: their dreadful solemnity and High Seriousness.
The Tenth Street *cénacle des cénacles* was full of artists
who were so *spiritual* that they never even got as far as
Pollock had in double-tracking out of the Boho Dance
and into the Consummation. They remained psychologically (and, by and by, resentfully) trapped in bohemia. Rothko refused to participate in a Whitney
Museum annual show in order to safeguard "the life my
pictures will lead in the world," and refused (or claimed

to refuse) to set foot in any Uptown art gallery unless some friend of his was having an opening. So Rauschenberg took to giving interviews in the art magazines in which he said that being an artist was no different, spiritually, from being a cargo humper or a file clerk or anything else. He exhibited *oeuvres* such as three Coca-Cola bottles, the actual bottles, surmounted by a pair of eagle wings. But all that was too easy to write off as mere Dada. Johns's 1958 show was something else again. It wasn't a coarse gesture; it was mighty cool . . . and something an ambitious young critic could fly with.

So Leo Steinberg, along with William Rubin, another theorist (and collector), depicted Johns's work as a newer, higher synthesis. The central arguing point? But of course—our old friend Flatness.

The new theory went as follows. Johns had chosen real subjects such as flags and numbers and letters and targets that were flat *by their very nature*. They were *born* to be flat, you might say. Thereby Johns was achieving an amazing thing. He was bringing real subjects into Modern painting but in a way that neither violated the law of Flatness nor introduced "literary" content. On the contrary: he was converting pieces of everyday communication—flags and numbers—into art objects . . . and thereby *de*-literalizing them! Were they content or were they form? They were neither! They were a higher synthesis. "An amazing result," said Steinberg.

Then Steinberg noticed something else. Johns had covered his flat signs in short, choppy Cézanne-like brushstrokes. Somehow this made them look flatter than ever . . . In fact, his flatness exposed once and for

Collection Mrs. Leo Castelli. Courtesy Leo Castelli Gallery

Jasper Johns's *Flag*, 1958. *Born* to be flat

all the *pseudo*-flatness of Abstract Expressionists like de Kooning and Pollock. The jig was up! Steinberg was now ready to give the *coup de grâce* to Clement Greenberg.

Greenberg had always argued that the Old Masters, the classic 3-D realists, had created "an illusion of space into which one could imagine oneself walking," whereas—to the everlasting glory of Modernism—you couldn't walk into a Modernist painting and least of all into an Abstract Expressionist painting. (Too honest, too flat for any such ersatz experience.) Just a minute, said Steinberg. That's all well and good, but you're talking about a "pre-industrial standard of locomotion," i.e., *walking*. Perhaps you can't *walk* into an Abstract Expressionist painting—but you can *fly* through. Right! You could take a spaceship! Just look at a de

Kooning or a Rothko or a Franz Kline. Look at that "airy" quality, those "areas floating in space," those cloud formations, all that "illusionistic space" with its evocations of intergalactic travel. Why, you could sail through a de Kooning in a Mercury capsule or a Soyuz any day in the week! All along, the Abstract Expressionists had been dealing in "open atmospheric effects." It was aerial "double dealing," and it did "clearly deny and dissemble the picture's material surface"—and nobody had ever blown the whistle on them!

Well, it was all now blown for Abstract Expressionism. Steinberg, with an assist from Rubin and from another theoretician, Lawrence Alloway, removed the cataracts from everybody's eyes overnight. Steinberg put across many of his ideas in a series of lectures at the Museum of Modern Art in 1960. The auditorium seats only 480, but with Cultureburg being such a small town—and the Museum looming so large in it—that platform was just right: his ideas spread as fast as Greenberg's had fifteen years before. Steinberg's manner was perfect for the new era. Where Greenberg was a theologian always on the edge of outrage and hostility, like Jonathan Edwards or Savonarola, Steinberg was cool, even a bit ironic. He was the young scholar, the historian; serious but urbane.

As soon as he realized what Johns's work meant, said Steinberg, "the pictures of de Kooning and Kline, it seemed to me, were suddenly tossed into one pot with Rembrandt and Giotto. All alike suddenly became painters of illusion." Later on, Steinberg changed that to "Watteau and Giotto"; perhaps for the crazy translingual rhyme, which, I must say, I like . . . or perhaps because being tossed into the same pot with Rembrandt, even by Leo Steinberg, was a fate that any artist, de Kooning included, might not mind terribly.

This may have been the end of Abstract Expressionism, but for Art Theory it was a fine, a rare, a beautiful, an *artistic* triumph. With that soaring aerial *aperçu* of Leo Steinberg's, Art Theory reached a heavenly plane, right up there with Paracelsus, Meister Eckhart, Christian Rosenkreutz, Duns Scotus, and the Scholastics . . . "How many angels can dance on the head of a pin?" That was once a question of infinite subtlety. Ah, yes! But consider: "Can a spaceship penetrate a de Kooning?"

Collection, The Museum of Modern Art, New York

Franz Kline's *Painting Number Two,* 1954.

Can a spaceship penetrate a Kline?

. . .

JASPER JOHNS'S SHOW WAS THE PERFECT EXHIBITION for the new age of Theory. He had intentionally devised it as an art lecture in pictures. It was like one of those puzzles in the 59-cent playbooks on sale in the wire racks in the supermarkets, in which you're invited to write down the sentences that the pictures create:

But wasn't there something just the least bit incestuous about this tendency of contemporary art to use previous styles of art as its point of reference? Early Modernism was a comment on academic realism, and Abstract Expressionism was a comment on early Modernism, and now Pop Art was a comment on Abstract Expressionism—wasn't there something slightly narrow, clubby, *ingrown* about it? Not at all, said Steinberg, whereupon he formulated one of the great axioms of the period: "Whatever else it may be, all great art is about art." Steinberg's evidence for this theory was far more subtle than convincing. *Sophistry,* I believe, is the word. He would cite Renaissance paintings with figures in the frames pointing at the main picture. (See? They're *commenting on* art.) But never mind . . . Steinberg's axiom was another one that inspired the profound *"That's . . . right!"* reaction throughout the art scene. Steinberg's own qualifier was dropped, and the *mot* became simply: "All great art is about art." That was like DDT for a lot of doubts that might otherwise have beset true believers over the next few years.

Meanwhile, Clement Greenberg and Harold Rosenberg made a grave tactical error. They simply denounced Pop Art. That was a gigantic blunder. Greenberg, above all, as the man who came up with the peerless Modern line, "All profoundly original work looks ugly at first," should have realized that in an age of avant-gardism no critic can stop a new style by meeting it head-on. To be against what is new is not to be modern. Not to be modern is to write yourself out of the scene. Not to be in the scene is to be nowhere. No, in an age of avant-gardism the only possible strategy to counter a new style which you detest is to *leapfrog* it. You abandon your old position and your old artists, leaping *over* the new style, land beyond it, point back to it, and say: "Oh, that's nothing. I've found something *newer* and *better* . . . way out here." This would dawn on Greenberg later.

Steinberg could attack Abstract Expressionism precisely because he was saying, "I've found something newer and better." But one will note that at no time does he attack the premises of Late-Twentieth-Century Art Theory as developed by Greenberg. He accepts every fundamental Greenberg has put forth. Realism and three-dimensional illusion are still forbidden. Flatness is still God. Steinberg simply adds: "I've found a new world that's flatter."

So that was how Pop Art came in: a new order, but the same Mother Church.

Within a few years the most famous images of Pop Art were Roy Lichtenstein's blowups of panels from war comics and love comics and Andy Warhol's Campbell's Soup cans and Brillo boxes. But wasn't that realism? Not at all. Quite the opposite, in fact. Alloway, the Englishman who coined the term *Pop Art,* provided the rationale: the comics, labels, and trademarks that the Pop artists liked were not representations of external reality. They were commonplace "sign systems" of American culture. By enlarging them and putting them on canvas, the artists were converting them from messages into something that was neither message nor external image. "Pop Art is neither abstract nor realistic," said Alloway, "though it has contacts in both directions. The core of Pop Art is at neither frontier; it is, essentially, an art about signs and sign systems." That may have been a bit hard to follow, but the stamp of approval came through clearly to one and all: "It's okay! You are hereby licensed to go ahead and like these pictures. We've drained all the realism out."

POP ART ABSOLUTELY REJUVENATED THE NEW YORK art scene. It did for the galleries, the collectors, the gallery-goers, the art-minded press, and the artists' incomes about what the Beatles did for the music business at about the same time. It was the thaw! It was spring again! The press embraced Pop Art with priapic delight. That goddamned Abstract Expressionism had been so solemn, so grim . . . "Shards of interpenetrated sensibility make their way, tentatively, through a not always compromisable field of cobalt blue—" How could you write about the freaking stuff? Pop Art you could have fun with.

Avant-gardism, money, status, Le Chic, and even the 1960s idea of sexiness—it all buzzed around Pop Art. *The* place, without any question, was Leo Castelli's gallery at 4 East Seventy-seventh Street. Castelli had Johns, Lichtenstein, Warhol, Robert Rauschenberg, James Rosenquist, most of the heavies. It was there that the Culture buds now hung out, beautiful little girls, with their hips cocked and the seams of their Jax slax cleaving them into hemispheres while they shot Culture pouts through their Little Egypt eyes.

God knows, the Pop artists themselves entered into the spirit of the thing. Whereas the Abstract Expressionists had so many disastrous problems double-tracking from the Boho Dance to the Consummation—whereas Pollock, Newman, Rothko, the whole push, in fact, had their own early antibourgeois boho ideals hovering over them forevermore like the most vengeful and vigilant superego in the history of psychology—the Pop artists double-tracked with about as much moral agony as a tape recorder. They came up with a new higher synthesis of personal conduct: to wallow in the luxuries of *le monde,* to junk it through with absolute abandon, was simply *part of the new bohemia*. Nothing to it! The artists used to hang around the apartment of Robert Scull, overlooking the Metropolitan Museum on Fifth Avenue, like children who don't know that you're supposed to go home at suppertime. They'd be there all afternoon, and Bob—Bob Scull—or Spike—Bob's wife, Ethel—he called her

Spike—would go around commenting on how it was getting dark and—oh, well, how about switching on a few lights, boys—and so they'd just turn on a few lights—and by and by it would be time to eat—and the artists would still be there, like little boys, wide-eyed and ready for goodies—and Spike would say, Well, we're going to eat now—and instead of saying, Uh, I guess I have to go home now, they'd say: Swell! Fine! Let's eat! (Where you taking us?) The only problem they had was that many of them were poor and plebeian in origin and had grown up in bohemia, and they didn't know even the rudimentary manners of life in *le monde,* but that didn't stop them for long. At first, Andy Warhol, for example, would go out to dinner and wouldn't know one end of that long lineup of silverware on the table from the other, and so he would sit there, at some five- or six-course dinner at the Burdens' or wherever, without touching a morsel, not the *crème sénégalaise* nor the lobster *cardinal* nor the veal *Valdostana* nor the salad Grant Street nor the fresh pear halves Harry & David—until finally the lady seated to his left would say, "But, Mr. Warhol, you haven't touched a thing!"—whereupon Andy would say, "Oh, I only eat candy." Warhol learned fast, however, and he soon knew how to take whatever he wanted. The bohemian, by definition, was one who did things the bourgeois didn't dare do. True enough, said Warhol, and he added an inspired refinement: nothing is more bourgeois than to be afraid to look bourgeois. True to his theory, he now goes about in button-down shirts, striped ties, and ill-cut tweed jackets, like a 1952 Holy Cross pre-med student. Warhol's ultimate liberation of the old puritanical Tenth Street boho ego, however, came the day he put an ad in *The Village Voice* saying that he would endorse anything, anything at all, for money . . . and listing his telephone number.

Double-tracking on all sides! Double-tracking at once naïve and infinitely subtle! Underneath the very popularity of Pop Art itself, as many people knew, and nobody said, was a deliciously simple piece of double-tracking. Steinberg, Rubin, and Alloway had declared Pop Art kosher and quite okay to consume, because it was all "sign systems," not realism. But everyone else, from the collectors to the Culture buds, was *cheating*!

They were like the Mennonite who, forbidden by religious law to have a TV set in his home, props it up on the fence post outside and watches through an open window. In the middle of January he sits in his living room huddled in an overcoat and a blanket, with the window open, because *Mannix* is out on the fence. In short . . . the culturati were secretly *enjoying the realism*!—plain old bourgeois mass-culture high-school goober-squeezing whitehead-hunting can-I-pop-it-for-you-Billy realism! They looked at a Roy Lichtenstein blowup of a love-comic panel showing a young blood couple with their lips parted in the moment before a profound, tongue-probing, post-teen, American soul kiss, plus the legend "WE ROSE UP SLOWLY . . . AS IF WE DIDN'T BELONG TO THE OUTSIDE WORLD ANY LONGER . . . LIKE SWIMMERS IN A SHADOWY DREAM . . . WHO DIDN'T NEED TO BREATHE . . ." and—the hell with the *sign systems*—they just loved the dopey campy picture of these two vapid blond sex buds having their love-comic romance bigger than life, six feet by eight feet, in fact, up

Private collection, Germany. Courtesy Leo Castelli Gallery

Roy Lichtenstein, "We Rose Up Slowly . . ." 1964.

Not realism . . . sign systems

on the walls in an art gallery. Dopey . . . campy . . . Pop Art was packed with literary associations, quite in addition to the love scene or whatever on the canvas. It was, from beginning to end, an ironic, a camp, a literary-intellectual assertion of the banality, emptiness, silliness, vulgarity, et cetera of American culture, and if the artists said, as Warhol usually did, "But that's what I like about it"—that only made the irony more profound, more cool.

Collectors and other culturati also liked this side of Pop Art immensely, because it was so familiar, so cozily antibourgeois, because once again it made them honorary congs walking along with the vanguard artists through the land of the philistines. Steinberg is the only theorist I know of, with the possible exception of

Bernard Berenson, who ever went to the trouble of creating some theory specifically for the passive role of consumer of culture. Were you upset by the swiftness of change? Did it worry you that one moment Abstract Expressionism was *it,* the *final style,* and then, in the blink of an eye, Abstract Expressionism was demolished and Pop Art was *it*? It shouldn't, said Steinberg—for that was precisely where the consumer of culture could show his courage, his mettle, his soldierly bearing. For what in the world requires more courage than "to applaud the destruction of values which we still cherish"? Modern Art always "projects itself into a twilight zone where no values are fixed," he said. "It is always born in anxiety." Not only that, he said, it is the very function of really valuable new Modern Art to "transmit this anxiety to the spectator," so that when he looks at it, he is thrown into "a genuine existential predicament." This was basically Greenberg's line, of course—"all profoundly original art looks ugly at first"—but Steinberg made the feeling seem deeper (and a bit more refined). The clincher was Steinberg's own confession of how he had at first disliked Johns's work. He had resisted it. He had fought to cling to his old values—and then realized he was wrong. This filtered down as a kind of Turbulence Theorem. If a work of art or a new style disturbed you, it was probably good work. If you *hated* it—it was probably *great.*

That was precisely the way Robert Scull discovered the artist Walter De Maria. Scull was walking down Madison Avenue on Saturday afternoon when he stopped in a gallery and saw some drawings that were nearly blank. They were pieces of drawing paper framed and hung, and down in one corner would be a few faint words, seemingly written by an ailing individual with a pencil so hard, a No. 8 or something, that the lead scarcely even made a line: "Water, water, water . . ." Scull hated these drawings so profoundly, he promptly called up the artist and became his patron. That brought De Maria his first recognition as a Minimal artist.

The Greatest Artist in the History of the World
collapses at the Automat

Up the fundamental aperture

INIMAL ART WAS PART OF A COMEBACK THAT AB-
stract art began to make, even while Pop Art was
still going strong. This time around, theory was
more dominant than ever.

I can remember the Museum of Modern Art an-
nouncing that it was going to have an exhibition in 1965
called "The Responsive Eye," a show of paintings with
special optical effects—what quickly became known as
Op Art. *Quickly* is hardly the word for it. A mad rush,
is more like it. Pop Art had been such a smashing success, with so many spin-offs, that it seemed like all of
smart New York was primed, waiting to see what the
art world would come up with next. By the time the
Museum's big Op Art show opened in the fall, two out
of every three women entering the glass doors on West

Collection, The Museum of Modern Art, New York

Bridget Riley, *Current*, 1964.

Not Op Art . . . Perceptual Abstraction

Fifty-third Street for the opening-night hoopla were wearing print dresses that were knockoffs of the paintings that were waiting on the walls inside. In between the time the show had been announced and the time it opened, the Seventh Avenue garment industry had cranked up and slapped the avant-garde into mass production before the Museum could even officially discover it. (They liked knocking off Bridget Riley's fields of vibrating lines best of all.)

Op, like Pop, was enjoyed for basically "literary" reasons. All of it, from Vasarely to Larry Poons, was reminiscent of the marvelous optical illusions in the syndicated newspaper feature "Ripley's 'Believe It or Not.' " But the *theory* of Op Art was something else. The Op artists never called it Op Art; they preferred Perceptual Abstraction. Their argument was: Cubism freed art from the nineteenth-century view of a painting as a window through which you saw an illusion of the real world. Earlier abstract work, such as De Stijl or Abstract Expressionism, had advanced this good work by establishing the painting as "an independent object as real as a chair or table" (to quote from "The Responsive Eye" catalogue). We Perceptual Abstractionists complete the process by turning this art object into a piece of pure perception. By creating special optical effects (but on a flat surface!) we remove it from the outside world and take it into that terra incognita "between the cornea and the brain."

Theory really started to roll now . . . toward reductionism. In this case: real art is nothing but what happens in your brain. Of course, Greenberg had started it all with his demands for purity, for flatness (ever more Flatness!), for the obliteration of distinctions such as foreground and background, figure and field, line and contour, color and pattern. Now, in the mid-1960s, Greenberg made a comeback.

He had learned a thing or two in the meantime about strategy. He no longer tried to defend Abstract Expressionism against the huge shift in taste that Pop Art represented. In fact, he offered what amounted to a piece of implied confession or, better said, self-criticism. All along, he said, there had been something old-fashioned about Abstract Expressionism, despite the many advances it brought. This old-fashioned thing was . . . its brushstrokes. Its *brushstrokes*? Yes, said Greenberg, its brushstrokes.* The characteristic Abstract Expressionist brushstroke was something very obvious, very expressive, very idiosyncratic . . . very *painterly,* like the "blurred, broken, loose definition of color and contour" you find in Baroque art. It was as obvious as a skid on the highway. He termed this stroke the "Tenth Street touch."

Lichtenstein, the Pop artist, liked this notion so much, or was so amused by it, that he did a series of *Brushstroke* paintings, each one a blowup of a single "Tenth Street touch" brushstroke, with every swirl and overloaded driblet represented—but rendered in the hard, slick commercial-illustration unpainterly style of Pop, with no brushstrokes of his own whatsoever to be seen.

Greenberg was still unbending in his opposition to Pop, but now he knew better than to just denounce it. Now he added the obligatory phrase: "—and I can show you something newer and better . . . way out here." This, he said, was Post-Painterly Abstraction.

Greenberg's Post-Painterly Abstraction has gone under other names since then: Hard-Edge-Abstract and Color Field Abstract, to name two. But all of them can be defined by the way in which they further the process of reduction, i.e., the way they get rid of something—just a little bit more, if you please! How far we've

---

* This was also an implicit criticism of his old rival, Rosenberg, the original prophet of the expressive brushstroke.

Lichtenstein's *Yellow and Red Brushstrokes,* 1966.

Brushstrokes without a single brushstroke showing; a flat picture of impasto and the old-fashioned Tenth Street past

come! How religiously we've cut away the fat! In the beginning we got rid of nineteenth-century storybook realism. Then we got rid of representational objects. Then we got rid of the third dimension altogether and got really flat (Abstract Expressionism). Then we got rid of airiness, brushstrokes, most of the paint, and the last viruses of drawing and complicated designs (Hard Edge, Color Field, Washington School).

Enough? Hardly, said the Minimalists, who began to come into their own about 1965. Bourgeois connotations, they argued, still hung on to Modern Art like a

necktie. What about all those nice "lovely" colors that
the Hard Edgers and the Color Fielders used? They invited as many sentimental associations as painterly
brushstrokes had. So Minimalists began using colors
like Tool & Die Works red and Subway I-Beam green
and Restaurant Exhaust-Fan Duct Lint gray that nobody could accuse of sentimentality. And how about all
those fuzzy, swampy, misty edges that Color Fielders

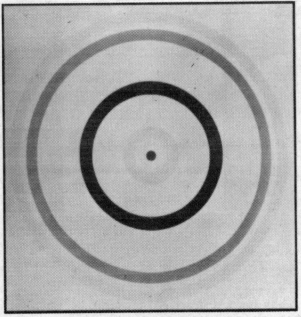

Collection, The Museum of Modern Art, New York

Kenneth Noland, *Turnsole*, 1961.

Noland was known as the *fastest* painter alive (i.e.,
one could see his pictures faster than anybody else's).
The explanation of why that was important took
considerably longer

like Olitski and Frankenthaler went for? They invited
you to linger over a painting for all its emotional "evocations," just like the worst junk of the old pre-
Raphaelites. Henceforth a paint should be applied only
in hard linear geometries, and you should get the whole
painting at once, "fast," to use the going phrase. (No
Loitering.) Kenneth Noland, formerly of Morris
Louis's misty Washington School, was now considered
the fastest painter in the business.

And how about the painting frame? Wasn't New
York full of artists who made a big thing about treating
the painting as an object—and then acted as if the
frame wasn't even there? So Frank Stella turned the
canvas itself into a frame and hung it on the wall with
nothing in the middle. That got rid of the frames, and
the era of "shaped canvases" began.

Sure, but what about this nice sweet bourgeois idea
of *hanging up pictures* in the first place ... all in their
nice orderly solid-burgher little rows? ... So artists like
Robert Hunter and Sol Lewitt began painting directly
on the gallery walls or on walls outside the gallery window ... with the faintest, most unsentimental geometric forms imaginable ...

FASTER AND FASTER ART THEORY FLEW NOW, IN
ever-tighter and more dazzling turns. It was dizzying,
so much so that both Greenberg and Rosenberg were
shocked—*épatés*. Greenberg accused the Minimalists of
living only for "the far-out as an end in itself." Their
work was "too much a feat of ideation ... something
deduced instead of felt and discovered." A little late to

be saying that, Clement! Rosenberg tried to stop them by saying they really weren't far-out at all—they were a fake avant-garde, a mere "DMZ vanguard," a buffer between the *real* avant-garde (his boy de Kooning) and the mass media. Very subtle—and absolutely hopeless, Harold! Theory, with a head of its own now, spun on and chewed up the two old boys like breadsticks, like the Revolution devouring Robespierre and Danton—faster and faster—in ever-tighter and more dazzling turns—let's see, we just got rid of the little rows of *hung pictures,* not to mention a couple of superannuated critics, and we've gotten rid of illusion, representational objects, the third dimension, pigment (or most of it), brushstrokes, and now frames and canvas—but what about the wall itself? What about the very idea of a work of art as something "on a wall" at all? How very pre-Modern! How can you treat the wall as something separate from the gallery, the room, the space in which it exists?

And so artists like Carl André, Robert Morris, Ronald Bladen, and Michael Steiner did huge geometric (unsentimental, uncolorful, fast) sculptures designed to divide up the entire gallery into spaces, to make the very building part of the sculpture in some way. No more "hanging" an exhibition; these were "installations."

But what about the very idea of the gallery or museum? What about the very notion of a nice sedate sanctum where one—meaning a person of the proper gentility—comes to gaze upon Art and the Artist with a glaze of respect and silence over his mug? Wasn't there something impossibly retrograde about the whole

Private collection, Beverly Hills. Courtesy Leo Castelli Gallery

Tampa (1964) by Frank Stella, who stood staunchly by the Word: fast, hard, flat, and unevocative, with paradise aforethought

thing? So began Earth Art, such as Michael Heizer's excavations in the dry lakes of the Mojave Desert and Robert Smithson's *Spiral Jetty* in the Great Salt Lake.

By now it was the late 1960s, and the New Left was in high gear, and artists and theorists began to hail Earth Art and the like as a blow against "the Uptown Museum-Gallery Complex," after the "military-industrial complex" out in the world beyond. If the capitalists, the paternalists of the art world, can't get their precious art objects into their drawing rooms or even into their biggest museums, they've *had it*. A few defiant notes like this, plus the signing of a few dozen manifestos against war and injustice—that was about as far as New York artists went into Left politics in the 1960s. With everyone now caught up in the spin of Theory, at such a furious velocity, the notion of putting on the brakes and doing that 1930s number again, cranking out some good old Social Realism propaganda, was too impossible to even think about. No, a few raspberries for the "museum-gallery complex" . . . and let's get back to business.

Back to business . . . which in the late 1960s was the monomaniacal task of *reduction*. What about the idea of a permanent work of art at all, or even a visible one? Wasn't that the most basic of all assumptions of the Old Order—that art was eternal and composed of objects that could be passed from generation to generation, like Columbus's bones? Out of that objection came Conceptual Art.

THE CONCEPTUALISTS LIKED TO PROPOUND THE FOL-lowing question: Suppose the greatest artist in the history of the world, impoverished and unknown at the time, had been sitting at a table in the old Automat at Union Square, cadging some free water and hoping to cop a leftover crust of toasted corn muffin or a few abandoned translucent chartreuse waxed beans or some other item of that amazing range of Yellow Food the Automat went in for—and suddenly he got the inspiration for the greatest work of art in the history of the world. Possessing not even so much as a pencil or a burnt match, he dipped his forefinger into the glass of water and began recording this greatest of all inspirations, this high point in the history of man as a sentient being, on a paper napkin, with New York tap water as his paint. In a matter of seconds, of course, the water had diffused through the paper and the grand design vanished, whereupon the greatest artist in the history of the world slumped to the table and died of a broken heart, and the manager came over, and he thought that here was nothing more than a dead wino with a wet napkin. Now, the question is: Would that have been the greatest work of art in the history of the world or not? The Conceptualists would answer: Of course, it was. It's not permanence and materials, all that Winsor & Newton paint and other crap, that are at the heart of art, but two things only: Genius and the *process* of creation! Later they decided that Genius might as well take a walk, too.

Conceptual Art divided into two sorts: things you could see, but not for long (like the Great Man's water picture), and things you couldn't see at all. From the first category came Peter Hutchinson's *Arc*. He filled some plastic bags with gas and pieces of rotten calabash or something of the sort, which was supposed to create more gas, tied the bags to a rope, put weights on either end of the rope, threw the whole business into the ocean, where the weights hit the bottom and the gas bags rose up, lifting the rope in an arc. An underwater photographer took pictures of the installation and then came back periodically to record the decay of the garbage and the eventual bursting of the bags and collapse of the arc—the disappearance of the art object, in short. Genius and process—process and genius! The photographs and quite a few lines of off-scientific prose provided the documentation, as it is known in Conceptual Art—which Hutchinson thereupon sold to the Museum of Modern Art for . . . well, today Museum officials prefer not to talk about how much they paid for *Arc.* One assumes that they paid no more than was necessary to remain buoyant in the turbulent intellectual waters of the late 1960s.

As for the second category—one of the great outposts of invisible Conceptual Art was the Richmond Art Center in Richmond, California, when Tom Marioni was its director. It was there that I came upon the fabulous *Beautiful Toast Dream,* by a woman whose name I can't remember. The documentation, which was typed, described how she woke up in the dark at about four in the morning and had a sudden craving for a piece of toast. The craving was so strong, in fact, that she could see it, a crust of Wonder Bread done light brown, and she could already visualize herself taking the crust out of the toaster and spreading Nucoa margarine on it with a serrated knife with a wooden handle, one of those slender numbers with little teeth on the blade that are good for cutting tomatoes or grapefruit, and she can see herself putting the Nucoa on the toast and then sprinkling some white sugar, the usual kind, on top of that and then shaking some cinnamon on it and then spreading it all on with the serrated knife until the heat of the toast begins to melt the margarine and the teeth of the knife begin to dig little furrows in the bread and the molten margarine begins to build up

ahead of each tooth and then runs off between the teeth
and into the furrows—but not by itself!—no, the margarine and little *ripped papillae of bread* run together
carrying with them on the surface of the tide granules
of sugar that absorb the molten margarine and turn yellow and disappear in this viscous flood of heat, steel,
and fragmented bread papillae while the cinnamon
maintains its spreckled identity except when bunching
up on the oleaginous surface of the flood like a stain
and the crest keeps building but becomes neither fluid
nor solid but more of a blob existing only as a kinetic
wobble swelling into one final macerated mulled mass
reflected in the stainless steel face of the blade as a
tawny cresting wave bound by an unbearable surface
tension until—all at once!—it is ripped, raked, rup-
tured by the blade and suddenly leaks as if through de-
flation between the teeth and into the lengthening
furrows behind the blade sinking lamely into a har-
rowed and utterly swamped tan bread delta and she
knows it is time to bite off a corner of the crust with yellow Nucoa-soaked sugar grains scraping the ridges of
her teeth and caking in the corners of her mouth—but
there were *no crusts to be found*—and she *could have no
toast*—and she had to have a swig of Diet-Rite Cola instead—and, well, I mean I can only *hint* at the tension,
the velocity, the suspense, the meth-like electron-
microscopic eye for detail and *le mot juste* that this
woman's documentation had—it went on and on; a
certain Frenchman would have given up the silence of
his cork-lined studio to have had *one-tenth* of this
woman's perception of the minutiae of existence or, in
this case, nonexistence, *one-twentieth* of her patience,

one-hundredth of her perseverance to stay with the description until the job is truly done—in short, I was in the presence of . . . *superb post-Proustian literature!*

With works such as that, late twentieth-century Modern Art was about to fulfill its destiny, which was: to become nothing less than Literature pure and simple. But the destined terminus had not yet been reached. After all, the artist of *Beautiful Toast Dream* had first gone through a visual experience, even if only imagined. After all, what about the whole business of "the visual imagination"? Came the refrain: How very pre-Modern.

David R. Smith (not the sculptor) tried to get rid of this, one of the last pieces of the old bourgeois baggage, through a piece called "Vacant":

VA   CA   NT

TN   AC   AV

Collection, Museum of Conceptual Art

—which was calculated to make the viewer concentrate on the utter emptiness between the letters. But he failed. He had still committed an act of visual imagination, even though in the service of invisibility, emptiness, nihilism. He had not gotten rid of the fundamental, the primary, the indigenous, the intrinsic, the built-in, the unitary and atomic impurity of the whole enterprise: namely, the artistic ego itself.

So it was that in April of 1970 an artist named Lawrence Weiner typed up a work of art that appeared in *Arts Magazine*—as a work of art—with no visual experience before or after whatsoever, and to wit:

1. The artist may construct the piece
2. The piece may be fabricated
3. The piece need not be built
Each being equal and consistent with the intent
of the artist the decision as to condition rests with
the receiver upon the occasion of receivership.

With permission, Arts Magazine

And there, at last, it was! No more realism, no more representational objects, no more lines, colors, forms, and contours, no more pigments, no more brushstrokes, no more evocations, no more frames, walls, galleries, museums, no more gnawing at the tortured face of the god Flatness, no more audience required, just a "receiver" that may or may not be a person or may or may not be there at all, no more ego projected, just "the artist," in the third person, who may be anyone or no one at all, for nothing is demanded of him, nothing at all, not even existence, for that got lost in the subjunctive mode—and in that moment of absolutely dispassionate abdication, of insouciant withering away, Art made its final flight, climbed higher and higher in an ever-decreasing tighter-turning spiral until, with one last erg of freedom, one last dendritic synapse, it disappeared up its own fundamental aperture . . . and came out the other side as Art Theory! . . . Art Theory pure and simple, words on a page, literature undefiled by vision, flat, flatter, Flattest, a vision invisible, even ineffable, as ineffable as the Angels and the Universal Souls.

Epilogue

FOR ABOUT SIX YEARS NOW, REALISTIC PAINTERS OF all sorts, real nineteenth-century types included, with 3-D and all the other old forbidden sweets, have been creeping out of their *Stalags,* crawl spaces, DP camps, deserter communes, and other places of exile, other Canadas of the soul—and have begun bravely exhibiting. They have been emboldened by what has looked to them, as one might imagine, as the modern art of Art Theory gone berserk.

The realist school that is attracting the most attention is an offshoot of Pop Art known as Photo-Realism. The Photo-Realists, such as Robert Bechtle and Richard Estes, take color photos of Pop-like scenes and objects—cars, trailers, storefronts, parking lots, motorcycle engines—then reproduce them precisely, in paint, on canvas, usually on a large scale, often by projecting them onto the canvas with a slide projector and then going to work with the paint. One of the things they manage to accomplish in this way, beyond the slightest doubt, is to drive orthodox critics bananas.

Such denunciations! "Return to philistinism"...

Collection Mr. and Mrs. Saul Steinberg. Courtesy Alan Stone Gallery

Richard Estes, *Bus Reflection*, 1972.

Perhaps the leading Photo-Realist, or at any rate the
most richly denounced; if the power to cause cortical
blowouts in critics is any recommendation,
he can't miss

"triumph of mediocrity" ... "a visual soap opera" ... "The kind of academic realism Estes practices might well have won him a plaque from the National Academy of Design in 1890" ... "incredibly dead paintings" ... "rat-trap compositional formulas" ... "its subject matter has been taken out of its social context and neutered" ... "it subjects art itself to ignominy" ... all quotes taken from reviews of Estes's show in New York last year ... and a still more fascinating note is struck: "This is the moment of the triumph of mediocrity; the views of the silent majority prevail in the galleries as at the polls."

Marvelous. We are suddenly thrust back fifty years into the mental atmosphere of Royal Cortissoz himself, who saw an insidious connection between the alien hordes from Southern Europe and the alien wave of "Ellis Island art." Only the carrier of the evil virus has changed: then, the subversive immigrant; today, the *ne kulturny* native of the heartland.

Photo-Realism, indeed! One can almost hear Clement Greenberg mumbling in his sleep: "All profoundly original art looks ugly at first ... but there is ugly and there is *ugly*!" ... Leo Steinberg awakes with a start in the dark of night: "Applaud the destruction of values we still cherish! But surely—not *this*!" And Harold Rosenberg has a dream in which the chairman of the Museum board of directors says: "Modernism is finished! Call the cops!"

Somehow a style to which they have given no support at all ("lacks a persuasive theory") is *selling*. "The New York galleries fairly groan at the moment under the weight of one sort of realism or another" ... "the incredible prices" ... Estes is reported to be selling at $80,000 a crack ... Bechtle for £20,000 at auction in London ... Can this sort of madness really continue "in an intellectual void"?

Have the collectors and artists themselves abandoned the very flower of twentieth-century art: i.e., Art Theory? Not yet. The Photo-Realists assure the collectors that everything is okay, all is kosher. They swear: we're not painting real scenes but, rather, camera images ("not realism, *photo systems*"). What is more, we don't show you a brushstroke in an acre of it. We're painting only scenes of midday, in bland sunlight—so as not to be "evocative." We've got all-over "evenness" such as you wouldn't believe—we put as much paint on that postcard sky as on that Airstream Silver Bullet trailer in the middle. And so on, through the checklist of Late Modernism. The Photo-Realists are backsliders, yes; but not true heretics.

In all of Cultureburg, in fact, there are still no heretics of any importance, no one attacking Late Modernism in its very foundation—not even at this late hour when Modern Art has reached the vanishing point and our old standby, Hilton Kramer, lets slip the admission: Frankly, these days, without a theory to go with it, I can't see a painting.

"LETS SLIP," AS I SAY. WE NOW KNOW, OF COURSE, that his words describe the actual state of affairs for *tout le monde* in Cultureburg; but it is not the sort of thing that one states openly. Any orthodox critic, such as Kramer, is bound to defend the idea that a work of art can speak for itself. Thus in December 1974 he attacked the curators of the Metropolitan Museum's exhibition "The Impressionist Epoch" for putting big historical notes up on the wall beside the great masterworks of the Impressionists. But why? What an opportunity he missed! If only he could have drawn upon the wisdom of his unconscious! Have the courage of your secret heart, Hilton! Tell them they should have made the copy blocks *bigger*!—and reduced all those Manets, Monets, and Renoirs to the size of wildlife stamps!

Twenty-five years from now, that will not seem like such a facetious idea. I am willing (now that so much has been revealed!) to predict that in the year 2000, when the Metropolitan or the Museum of Modern Art puts on the great retrospective exhibition of American Art 1945-75, the three artists who will be featured, the three seminal figures of the era, will be not Pollock, de Kooning, and Johns—but Greenberg, Rosenberg, and Steinberg. Up on the walls will be huge copy blocks, eight and a half by eleven feet each, presenting the protean passages of the period . . . a little "fuliginous flatness" here . . . a little "action painting" there . . . and some of that "all great art is about art" just beyond. Beside them will be small reproductions of the work of leading illustrators of the Word from that period, such as Johns, Louis, Noland, Stella, and Olitski. (Pollock and de Kooning will have a somewhat higher status, although by no means a major one, because of the more symbiotic relationship they were fortunate enough to enjoy with the great Artists of the Word.)

Every art student will marvel over the fact that a whole generation of artists devoted their careers to getting the Word (and to internalizing it) and to the extra-ordinary task of divesting themselves of whatever there was in their imagination and technical ability that did not fit the Word. They will listen to art historians say, with the sort of smile now reserved for the study of Phrygian astrology: "That's how it was then!"—as they describe how, on the one hand, the scientists of the mid-twentieth century proceeded by building upon the dis-coveries of their predecessors and thereby lit up the sky . . . while the artists proceeded by averting their eyes from whatever their predecessors, from da Vinci on, had discovered, shrinking from it, terrified, or dis-integrating it with the universal solvent of the Word. The more industrious scholars will derive considerable pleasure from describing how the art-history professors and journalists of the period 1945–75, along with so many students, intellectuals, and art tourists of every sort, actually struggled to *see* the paintings directly, in the old pre–World War II way, like Plato's cave dwellers watching the shadows, without knowing what had projected them, which was the Word.

What happy hours await them all! With what snig-gers, laughter, and good-humored amazement they will look back upon the era of the Painted Word!

OTHER PICADOR BOOKS
AVAILABLE FROM PAN MACMILLAN

TOM WOLFE

FROM BAUHAUS TO OUR HOUSE	0 330 32609 0	£5.99
HOOKING UP	0 330 48611 X	£6.99
KANDY-KOLORED		
TANGERINE FLAKE BABY	0 330 26525 3	£6.99
BONFIRE OF THE VANITIES	0 330 29633 7	£7.99
THE RIGHT STUFF	0 330 31819 5	£7.99
THE NEW JOURNALISM	0 330 24315 2	£8.99

All Pan Macmillan titles can be ordered from our website,
www.panmacmillan.com, or from your local bookshop
and are also available by post from:

Bookpost, PO Box 29, Douglas, Isle of Man IM99 1BQ
Credit cards accepted. For details:
Telephone: 01624 836000
Fax: 01624 670923
E-mail: bookpost@enterprise.net
www.bookpost.co.uk

Free postage and packing in the United Kingdom

Prices shown above were correct at the time of going to press.
Pan Macmillan reserve the right to show new retail prices on covers
which may differ from those previously advertised in the text
or elsewhere.